sex adviser

sex adviser

the 100 most asked questions about sex between men

tony palermo

alyson books
los angeles | new york

MANUFACTURED IN THE UNITED STATES OF AMERICA.

THIS TRADE PAPERBACK ORIGINAL IS PUBLISHED BY ALYSON PUBLICATIONS INC.,
P.O. BOX 4371, LOS ANGELES, CALIFORNIA 90078-4371.
DISTRIBUTION IN THE UNITED KINGDOM BY TURNAROUND PUBLISHER SERVICES LTD.,
UNIT 3 OLYMPIA TRADING ESTATE, COBURG ROAD, WOOD GREEN, LONDON N22 6TZ ENGLAND.

FIRST EDITION: JANUARY 1999

03 02 01 00 99   10 9 8 7 6 5 4 3 2 1

ISBN 1-55583-485-X

ALL MATERIAL ORIGINALLY PUBLISHED IN UNZIPPED. REPRINTED WITH PERMISSION OF LIBERATION PUBLI-
CATIONS INC.

To Robrt L. Pela and John Erich.
Without them, I'm nothing.

contents

introduction

If I had a dime for every time a gay man asked me why his butt is bleeding…well, I wouldn't need to write a sex-advice column for a living. But as it turns out, my job as the Sex Adviser has netted me more than a paycheck every couple of weeks. I have—thanks to the sexy subject matter of the letters I receive—learned more about life than I would have in any other job I can imagine.

Because that's the thing about sex: It's really just a barometer of our lives—or the way we think we'd like to be living. A letter from a guy who's married and is secretly lusting after the UPS man is really his first step in coming out to himself and getting out of a rotten situation. And when some kid writes from the sticks asking how to break into the porn business, he's really pining for a life away from the horrors of heartless parents and farm chores and the isolation of feeling like the only gay kid in the world.

Before I ruin my reputation as a sarcastic know-it-all with any more of this pretentious sex-as-life crap, let me tell you that being the guy with all the sex answers has other, more trivial advantages. For one thing, being the Sex Adviser has made me hugely popular at parties. Folks are forever abandoning the hors d'oeuvres tray to inquire about my most-asked question ("Where can I go to meet someone like me?"), the weirdest question I've been asked ("How can I produce more head cheese more quickly?"), and the strangest letter I've ever received (one from a man in my hometown wanting advice on how to introduce himself to a guy he'd been admiring from afar who, unbeknownst to him, was *me*). And if cute guys want to come on to me because they think that being a sexpert means I'll be great in bed, I let them.

But if this is the best job I've ever had, it's not because of the attention it bags me at parties or because I get to work in my boxers from the comfort of my own home. The real advantage to being the queer Ann Landers is that it's finally proved to me that there *is* some unity among gay men. I've been to gay pride rallies and read queer manifestos, and none of it ever convinced me that there's anything to this "gay community" concept. But once you've read 400 letters from 400 guys all asking why the heck it's so hard to find love, you realize that our unity is grounded not in the rainbow-flag bumper stickers on our cars but in our similar stories. Most of us have the same struggles—to get laid, to come out or stay in the closet, to choose a new wallpaper pattern—and it's these common travails that unite us.

The other thing we appear to have in common is the inability to tell our doctors about that pesky rash in our trousers. In closing, I'd like to repeat, for the hundredth time, three last things: Your doctor doesn't care about your sex life; your parents already know you're gay, even if you haven't told them; and no, it is *not* a good idea to tell your boss that you're wearing women's lingerie under your Brooks Brothers.

Tony Palermo
October 1998

chapter 1

cocks

1}

Is it true that uncut penises are usually longer than cut ones? I read someplace that this is true, but I find it hard to believe. Also, why is it that guys who appear in magazines always pull back their foreskins for pictures? Any insight you can offer would be appreciated.

Penises with long foreskins tend to look longer than circumcised penises for the simple reason that there's more stuff hanging there. A long, dangling foreskin can add another half an inch to any cock, which (as we all know) is actually two inches when we're doing the measuring.

There are innumerable reasons models pull back their foreskins in photographs. Here are some of my favorites, in no particular order:

• The men in question want you to see what the heads of their penises look like. When they're swathed in foreskin, men's meat can't be fully admired.

• While some men have eroticized foreskin and like the

look of that extra flap of skin, others find foreskins repellent. A model with an uncircumcised penis has the opportunity for two different "looks" during a photo shoot. This way he's presumably twice as appealing.

• Just as some guys like models who play with their nipples, others dig shots of men yanking back their extra dick skin on-camera. You can bet that right this very minute there's some hot stud holding up a copy of *Foreskin Quarterly* with one paw and hollering, "Yeah, baby! Pull back that cheesy foreskin! Come on. Pull it back…"

2}

To put it bluntly, I am having a problem with my penis. When I am naked in public and get nervous, my penis shrinks up so that it looks very small or even nonexistent. This is embarrassing to me because I belong to some gay nudist groups. However, it is even more of a problem because for fun, I used to like to pose nude for drawing classes at local art schools. I am reluctant to do this now because I don't want the students to think that I don't have a dick.

This never used to be a problem; it started only a few years ago. I was a student taking figure-drawing classes at a local school. I had posed nude several times before when the model hadn't shown up. One evening when the model didn't show, I was a bit nervous about volunteering because I had recently heard one of the other male students make some jokes about the bodies of other models. However, I went ahead and posed anyway. But because I was self-conscious, my dick shrank up.

The few times I have posed since then, I start out by being afraid that it is going to shrink up, which then causes that very thing to happen (even though the aforementioned student is no longer around). Is there anything I can do to solve this problem? I have thought of three ideas: hypnosis, erection cream, and a vacuum pump. What do you suggest?

I suggest you forget all about long-term solutions to your short-term problem. Erection cream is snake oil, and measures as drastic as a penis pump may give you a bigger dick but won't solve your problem—bigger dicks can shrink up in public too.

There's a quicker and less-taxing solution to your predicament: Since every man's penis is larger just after erection, the best time to show off your flaccid penis is in its post-tumescent state. The penile sock remains stretched for a time after erection, giving your dick more length and girth.

Shortly before you're set to pose, fantasize about something sexy—Tom Cruise boffing Brad Pitt, for example, or maybe a scene from your favorite porn film. After your dick gets hard, switch gears and think about your mother, your tax return, or Jayne Mansfield in a teddy. Barring any drafts, your newly soft dick will remain at its longest flaccid state for up to half an hour.

You seem to like being seen naked, which suggests that you're proud of your body. You might spend some time in front of the mirror focusing on those parts of your body you're more comfortable showing off. Commend yourself on the enormous bravery it takes to stand naked in front of a roomful of people. And remind yourself that in the end the size of your dick while you're posing for a drawing class is secondary to everyone but you.

3}

Because I have a small penis, I suffer from depression and other anxiety disorders. I am 3½ inches hard and almost nonexistent soft. I have had a life of misery because of this problem, and no one even seems to care. I've been mistreated and degraded all of my life because I am so small.

I've sought professional help and have been mistreated there also. I don't know what to do anymore and have basically given up on ever having a relationship. I can't even leave my room because of the stigma of having a small penis.

Recently an ad about penile enlargement ran in my local newspaper, and I thought my life would finally change. Now I've heard that all the claims being made about this procedure are bogus, and I'm once again in a depressed state. I don't have any friends and feel like my life is over at 24. It would be great to know that others share my problem and that there's someone I can talk to about this.

There *are* professionals to whom you can speak about your problem, and I urge you to seek out one of them right away. You may have had a crummy experience with counseling in the past, but that shouldn't stand in the way of your seeking real help now. Knowing that you're a whole person regardless of the length and girth of your organs is vital—and a difficult knowledge to gain. A counselor or social worker (who, by the way, has no interest in how big you are) can assist you in finding ways to feel right about yourself regardless of what you feel you lack physically.

By the way, there are safe, effective, non-surgical ways to lengthen your penis. Most of them have been documented by Added Dimensions Publishing in one or more of their many books on penis enlargement. You can call Added Dimensions at (619) 770-9647 or write them at 100 S. Sunrise Way, Suite 484, Palm Springs, CA 92263 to request a catalog. But remember, the size of your wink is never as important as the size of your self-esteem.

Finally, please know that as hard as it may be to believe, there are men out there to whom the size of your cock is unimportant.

4}

All my life I have suffered from feelings of inadequacy. Perhaps that is why I always give rather than receive oral sex. Many men and women come over to my place solely to get serviced, then they leave. I have come to accept this behavior rather than reveal my deepest, darkest secret: I have a small dick. In fact, I have told these people that I am impotent to forestall any reciprocation on their part.

Even as a teenager I picked activities in high school that would not require undressing. That is why I got out of gym and joined the band. As an adult I went briefly to a gym, but changing there was so difficult for me (showering was out of the question) that I stopped going.

I prefer not even telling you how small my dick is when it's soft. Being generous, I would say I'm about five inches when hard. When I was 12, everything shot up: I grew six inches and started to fill out, and puberty hit—but my penis stayed the same. It's not

a topic one goes to one's parents about. That is why I continue even to this day to suffer with these feelings. Many times I have contemplated suicide to end my suffering.

I am turning to you not as a last resort but because I can remain anonymous. Outside of therapy, which I refuse to do, do you know of any support organizations for bisexual men who aren't hung like horses? With your vast knowledge of sex-related groups and materials, I plead with you to end the suffering and endless humiliation I feel over having a small dick.

Forget about support groups for bisexual men with small dicks. Whoever or whatever convinced you that you need a humongous dick to be a complete man did you a great disservice. The facts of the matter are: 1) You're not that small; and 2) So what if you were?

Depending on whom you ask, an average dick is considered to be about 5½ to six inches long, so while you may be a bit smaller than average, you are by no means freakishly tiny. In my own personal sexual experience, I have encountered dozens of men who are smaller than you. The ones who knew how to use what they had were good sexual partners, and neither of us were hung up on dick size. Conversely, I've also been with men with bigger dicks who were not good lovers. There will always be size queens who hold that bigger is better, but they are, for the most part, a minority. I've heard many others actually express preferences for nice "mouth-size" cocks.

It's natural for teenagers to feel insecure and inadequate about their bodies, but it is unnatural to maintain those feelings into adulthood. For whatever reason, you have been unable to let go of those adolescent insecurities. Like it or not, counseling is probably what you need. A trained medical professional should neither judge nor belittle you and, in fact, will be better informed and equipped to help you than any gay-smut advice columnist.

There are ways to increase your dick size (weights, vacuum pumps, enhancement surgery) that have been discussed here before, but that's not the course of action I recommend for you. You need to realize that the measure of a dick is not the measure of a man. Please give counseling a chance—it beats the heck out of self-pity.

5}

For as long as I can remember, I've wished for a larger and longer penis. I'm not the smallest guy I've ever seen, but I've always felt inadequate. These feelings first took root when I was in junior high school gym class, and I've been embarrassed about my size ever since. Erect, I am about 5½ inches in length and 4½ inches in circumference.

I tried an expensive vacuum pump, and that increased my circumference by about half an inch. Then I decided I'd like to stretch my foreskin with the cone system—I now have loose skin that almost covers the glans when I'm erect. I thought foreskin would make me more interesting, since I feel that everyone is looking for a large box and that obviously isn't going to happen for me.

As if that weren't enough, I then read an article about penile elongation through use of a strap with weights worn twice daily for up to 20 minutes. This is where the dilemma comes in: I followed the directions and seemed to gain about half an inch in length, making me six inches. I also started to have a veiny appearance, which I enjoyed. But then I noticed that I was losing sensation in the glans of my penis. I stopped using the weights, of course, but it's very difficult to reach orgasm now.

I have begun to realize that the size and shape of my penis are not as important as the enjoyment I once had. I have spent nearly $1,000 to learn this lesson, and now I fear the nerve damage may be permanent. Please consult your references and colleagues—is there any hope of restoring sensation to my dick? Please print this letter so your readers can understand the potential consequences of home penile enlargement and enhancement techniques. All I have managed to obtain in three years of work is minimal gain and a loss of sensation.

Thanks for sharing what must be an embarrassing problem. I hope our readers will pay attention and learn what you discovered the hard way.

The decreased sensation you describe is probably the result of nerve damage in your glans. Nerves in this area (and in your other extremities) are called peripheral nerves, and while they're more likely to regenerate themselves than nerves in areas such as the brain or spinal cord, they nonetheless are not indestructible. You should see a urologist for an evaluation of how much damage you've sustained and possible methods of treatment. The essence of treatment will likely entail avoiding further damage and allowing your body to heal itself.

Some urologists specialize in penile enhancement, but no such procedure is without risk. For example, the suspensory ligament, which is located in the pelvis above the base of the penis, can be cut. This will allow that part of the penile structure that is usually suspended within the pelvis to drop out, causing the penis to dangle longer. You will gain length but lose elevation in your erection; that is, your dick will still get hard, but it won't point as high. Many urologists, however, will not perform this procedure.

To increase girth, some urologists will inject fat into the penis shaft, boosting the circumference. This sounds good, but sometimes the fat will clump up under the skin, forming hard, unsightly deposits. Some experts also expect the fat to be reabsorbed by the body over time, negating any gains.

The lesson here is this: Love yourself for who you are! Changing your dick size isn't like dying your hair or trying to drop a few pounds—those are cosmetic changes that shouldn't affect your long-term health. Your dick is something nature gave you; its size and shape are determined by genes, and if your genes meant you to have more, then you'd have more. This also goes for cut guys trying to create foreskins and uncut guys trying to get rid of them. All dicks are lovely in their own ways, so leave that thing alone.

6}

In my short experience with men, I have noticed something peculiar about some men's genitals: Some are decidedly darker in color than the rest of the body. I refer you to the bedroom scene at the end of the film *Maurice.* When Alec (Rupert Graves) walks across the room to put on his clothes, he is completely naked. I was struck by the fact that his genitals are so dark in color that they look almost as if they do not belong to him.

This is not the only time I have seen such a thing. My friend Bob is blond and very fair in complexion. Yet his genitals are incredibly dark, so much so that if you were to photograph just his cock and balls, you would swear they belonged to a black man. I find the above quite bizarre and am curious about how such a thing comes about. One person suggested circumcision might be the cause, but that can't be the case. Graves was definitely uncircumcised, and Bob is cut. I don't want to make a big deal out of this, but I'd like to know how it happens.

The color and size of the genitals are regulated by our genes, much like the color of our eyes, height, and hair color and texture. The striking difference that you mention has survived in the gene pool because it does not interfere with breeding (which passes on the trait). In fact, in some cultures such interesting genitals might even draw more attention to their owner and increase his chances of reproducing. It's hard to say just how unusual it is, though, because of our society's strictures against public nudity. Just about the only place you can see a lot of naked men is in pornography, and that is hardly a representative sample, since porn producers reject anybody who isn't well-hung. A very dark or very light dick that didn't match a model's skin tones might be rejected as well— or make him a big star, depending on the producer's foibles.

Your reaction to men with harlequin-style cocks seems to be based in part on some interesting racial stereotypes. I'm not calling you a racist. Certain attitudes about racial differences are so deeply ingrained in our culture that it's hard to ferret them out. A racial dichotomy of black and white necessarily has to be based on the idea that human beings can be neatly divided into dark- and light-skinned people. Intermediate types who can't be immediately placed in one category or the other throw us off. But, in fact, nature doesn't mind at all if people combine different racial characteristics. We are the ones who get tweaked and think it's weird. We are the ones who have connected skin color to a host of other assumptions about intelligence, income, aggression, independence, and more. Race is an idea, a belief, not a biological imperative.

7}

My circumcised penis is very small when soft but stretches to an average-size six-inch erection. I'm less concerned about my size than I am the bluish color of the underside of the tip. This area has been there ever since I can remember and is cold to the touch when not erect and is basically numb. Does this mean I have poor circulation? I know some people sometimes have toes amputated because of poor circulation, and I wonder if my penis is in danger of a similar fate. I am 30 years old, not overweight, don't have diabetes or other health problems, and have not had any trauma to my penis. None of my other extremities are blue.

Before I offer the usual mound of advice and assurance, let me thank you for the delightful sketch of your penis that you included at the bottom of your letter. I'm assuming from your description of yourself that this large and enticing illustration was not drawn to actual scale.

As long as you haven't been mishandling your dick, you

needn't worry about losing any part of it. The cold bluish spot on the underside of your dick is probably nothing more than a birthmark. Permanent irregularities to the skin don't receive the same blood flow as the rest of our epidermis. If the spot is cold when your dick is flaccid and warm when you're hard, it's probably because there's more blood flowing to your cock when you have an erection and anything attached to your dick at that time is going to heat up considerably. (In fact, I'm getting hard just thinking about it.)

If you're feeling especially bitter, you may want to blame your condition on Jewish tradition. After circumcision some areas of the penis are rendered permanently numb by a buildup of scar tissue. Likewise, other areas are so sensitive that any other place on your dick seems anesthetized in comparison.

If I seem unconcerned or flippant about the dot on your dick, it's primarily because you mention having had it ever since you can remember. If your little blue spot has been there all along and you haven't had any problems connected with it, relax. Point it out to your regular physician the next time you're getting a physical, and keep an eye on it to make sure it doesn't grow. Meanwhile, you might consider using it as part of your seduction technique. You can tell your next trick, "The end of my dick is kind of cold. Maybe you could put it in your mouth and warm it up a little."

8}

I am an 18-year-old gay male who is concerned with pain and discomfort at the base of my penis and scrotum. When I have an erection, my penis follows parallel to my stomach and navel, touching my stomach. During my first sexual experience, I had a lot of discomfort during oral and anal sex. I just assumed that it was because I was a virgin, but twice since the first time I have had the same problem happen again. I have noticed that my friends' erections are different from mine. Their penises point straight out from their bodies, whereas mine points straight up against my body. Do I have a severe problem? Should I consult a doctor?

It would be foolish for me to try to diagnose a medical problem through the mail. I also can't gauge its severity. This could be something minor and easy to fix or something more serious. You should make an appointment with a doctor and get checked out. The kind of pain you describe is not normal. You shouldn't have to put up with that every time you have sex.

Maybe you are reluctant to see a doctor because you don't want to describe a sexual problem. Perhaps you don't have a physician who is knowledgeable about gay sexuality and positive about us. I urge you to conquer whatever fear or embarrassment you have and seek medical attention despite your discomfort. You don't need to tell the doctor you are gay or mention the gender of your sexual partners. Straight men also have oral sex and anal sex. The doctor may not even need to know these details; he or she may simply need to give you a physical examination.

This really is something you should not neglect. Problems like this usually don't go away if you ignore them. Instead, they often become worse. If you are unlucky and get a doctor who is negative or not helpful, just try again until you find somebody sympathetic. Gay people often neglect their health issues because of homophobia in the medical profession. But there are caring, non-judgmental health care practitioners out there, so get connected with somebody who can help you stay well.

9}

When I was a boy, I was an oddity among my peers—I am uncircumcised. I was never ridiculed or in any way made to feel like an outcast, but nevertheless I felt compelled to alter this condition. Perhaps it just seemed sexier to be circumcised like all my friends were. Anyway, after discovering and removing some buildup of smegma from under my foreskin, I found it easy to train my foreskin to stay rolled back from the glans, thus creating the appearance of being circumcised, and it has remained so ever since. But now that I desire to train my foreskin to cover the glans, it stubbornly rolls itself back only minutes after I have stretched it over the head. I have even tried wrapping a rubber band around the stretched foreskin to keep it there, but that was too painful to endure. The head of my cock is a bit larger in circumference than the shaft. Am I destined to forever regret my childhood need for conformity, or is there some way to return my foreskin to its original state?

If men who have been circumcised can benefit from a program of foreskin restoration, surely it will work for you, who wants only to stretch his 'skin back to its starting position. You can order Gary Griffin's *Decircumcision*, a book that describes the process, by sending a check or money order for $9.95, plus $5 for shipping and handling, to Second Skin, 521 St. Phillips St., New Orleans, LA 70116. (Residents of Texas, Louisiana, Arkansas, and Mississippi should add 4% sales tax.) Second Skin also sells foreskin restoration cones, which can be used to stretch your foreskin with a minimum of discomfort.

There's something really crazy about a society that abhors the penis in its natural state. One of these days circumcision is going to be viewed as a barbaric anachronism every bit as cruel (and widespread at one time) as foot-binding. I don't think men who were cut should feel bad about their genitals, but I wonder what the widespread psychological effects of mass partial castration have been on too many generations of American men. It's great that you are trying to undo the ill effects of that childhood spate of self-hatred.

chapter 2

coming out

10}

I am a 29-year-old who until recently was hidden away in the closet. I have come out now, but I still feel that there is a lot to learn about the gay lifestyle. To start with, I was wondering about the different gay symbols: the rainbow, the lambda, and others. I was wondering if you could explain the symbolic significance for each of them as well as the history behind them. I was also wondering if you could tell me some good books to read that would also help me in better understanding things like that as well as getting a better understanding of our gay history. I would appreciate any assistance you could give me in my endeavor to learn more about the lives and history of gays everywhere.

The most prominent and most often seen of our symbols are the lambda, the pink triangle, and the rainbow flag. The last of these has taken on numerous (and increasingly scary) commercial connotations lately, most notably as freedom-ring necklaces and most recently as those rainbow decals that so many rear bumpers seem to be sporting these days.

The rainbow flag—designed by Gilbert Baker of San Francisco in 1978—was originally intended to represent the diversity of the gay and lesbian community. And before it was a key chain, the lambda was merely a letter of the Greek alphabet. It was chosen by the Gay Activists Alliance in 1970 as a symbol of the gay movement.

The pink triangle is the most controversial of our images. It was originally employed by the Nazis to designate homosexuals in World War II concentration camps. The pink triangle, with one tip pointing down, was sewn onto the clothing of known homosexuals, who were singled out for mistreatment. Gay activists adopted the symbol in the 1970s to call attention to this horrifying chapter of gay history.

Your local gay bookshop is bursting with entertaining and enlightening literature. Try Martin Duberman's *Stonewall*, which provides insight into the era preceding the modern gay rights movement. *The Alyson Almanac* and Leigh Rutledge's *The Gay Fireside Companion* are both great quick-reference books. And don't overlook historical fiction either; several significant works have captured periods of our history and culture. Andrew Holleran's *Dancer From the Dance* is a wonderfully written and entertaining peek at the '70s sex-and-disco scene, and Edmund White's *The Beautiful Room Is Empty* tells the story of one young man's pre-Stonewall coming-out.

Finally, let me point out that there is no such thing as

the "gay lifestyle" any more than there is a nongay lifestyle. You're not bound by anyone else's concept of what gay men do or should be. You set the limits and boundaries that feel right for you and take it from there. Welcome to the fold.

11}

I never imagined myself writing to you for help, but now I am forced to do so. I recently turned 18, and I'm the only openly gay male at my high school. Many people ask me, "How do you know you're gay if you haven't had sex with another man?" My response to that is, "How do you know you're straight if you haven't had sex with a member of the opposite sex?"

Nevertheless, this question has always sparked some curiosity on my part. Although I haven't had sex with a man, I am thinking about it constantly. I am eagerly awaiting my first encounter; however, I am also very anxious about it. I'm afraid that I might contract a disease, that I might suck his dick the wrong way, or that I might get hurt during intercourse. To make matters worse, I can't find any support groups for gay teenagers in the St. Louis area. I'm about ready to give up and join a monastery.

Forget about the cloister. All those Hollywood nun movies make it look glamorous, but do you really want to have your head shaved and be renamed Sister Mary Teen Libido?

It's perfectly natural that you're worried about your first time. Sex is like playing with a yo-yo: You get better at it the more you do it. If you're brave enough to come out to your school pals, you're brave enough to seduce a man. Start slowly, use lots of lube and stacks of condoms, and remember: Keep your teeth out of the way when you're sucking his dick.

Read *Gay Sex* by Jack Hart for pointers on what to do and how to do it. A couple of porn flicks will help build your bedroom repertoire, and talking to your partner about what he likes to do before climbing into bed with him won't hurt.

There are other inquisitive, horny teens in your area. Some of them meet under the auspices of Growing American Youth, an organization for young gays and lesbians in St. Louis. Call them at (314) 533-5322 for information on their next meeting. Good luck, and welcome to the fold.

12}

At 30 years of age I am still confused about my sexual preference. I had a few homosexual experiences as a teenager, but since then I've been strictly heterosexual—until recently. Lately I've been buying your magazine and even a few gay videos. I guess my question is, Should I explore this possibility or just stay straight? Also, how do I meet men in my area and be discreet about finding a same-sex lover? Any information or advice would be greatly appreciated.

What is this, a trick question? You're writing to a gay magazine, so I'm not likely to tell you that homosexuality is dirty and sinful and wrong. What I'm going to tell you is to get out there and try to figure out what it is you want.

Maybe you're gay and just now realizing it, or maybe you're straight and just a little curious, but you'll never know unless you investigate. A little cautious experimentation never hurt anybody, and in your case it could go a long way toward putting your mind at ease. So find yourself a man and find out what feels comfortable to you. Bars, gyms, and certain publications in the nearest large city are good places to start.

From the way you portray your situation, I suspect that you're gay (or, at the very least, bisexual) and have just been repressing it for lo these many years. If you have a sexual attraction to men, as your interest in magazines and videos suggests you do, then denying it is a recipe for a lifetime of unhappiness. You gotta be you. Good luck.

13}

I am an Asian guy in my late 20s who's been in the United States for two years. I am miserable. I believe I am bisexual because I am attracted to both sexes. I find men attractive and fantasize about them, but I have never had any physical contact with another man. I just can't afford to come out of the closet. My family is very conservative. They love me, but I am positive they won't accept my true sexuality. I don't want them to disown me.

These feelings became so overwhelming in my teens that I attempted suicide. My parents thought it was an accident. I don't know how long I can hide my real identity, and it scares me. Perhaps through your column I can find someone to correspond with who will understand me.

It is important for you to take the amount of stress that you are feeling very seriously. Since you attempted suicide once already, you are at an increased risk of attempting it again. Which is better to risk—your family's disapproval or death? There is nothing wrong with who you are. Society may disapprove and people may not understand, but you have an innate capacity to love and desire other men, and that need is healthy and correct for you.

You can get more information about your sexuality and obtain some support without coming out to your family. In fact, I would advise you to put off telling them for as long as possible. I think you need a therapist who will help you to explore all your options and keep the level of stress in your life as low as possible. Unfortunately, I can't locate any gay services in the North Florida area. But there are gay agencies nearby that may have more comprehensive information.

Jacksonville has a touch-tone database for the gay community. Call (904) 396-8044. There's also a gay switchboard in Gainesville at (904) 332-0700. These folks can help you to get a better picture of your local community and connect you with a counselor. They can also tell you where to go to buy gay books and magazines so you can start learning about gay history and culture. Perhaps there is even a coming-out group you could join.

I can't help you to find a pen pal by publishing your address in this column. But you can find someone to write to by placing your own personal ad. Rent a post office box and specify that they accept mail in your legal name and in an alias, or use the magazine's mail-forwarding service to protect your true identity. You can also find a pen pal through International Gay Penpals, P.O. Box 7304 #320, North Hollywood, CA 91603 or United Brothers, P.O. Box 1733, Louisville, KY 40201. I also recommend the gay

South Asian publication *Trikone,* P.O. Box 21354, San Jose, CA 94151; (408) 270-8776.

Remember that the journey to understanding one's own sexuality is lifelong. Be patient with yourself. Don't feel that you have to rush into anything or do something self-destructive. For now it's important to just gather information, find some sympathetic people to talk to who will respect your privacy, and end your isolation. The day may come when you have so many gay or bisexual friends—perhaps even a boyfriend—that you feel safe confronting your family. In the meantime, stall them. Until you are sure of your sexual orientation, don't get married. The misery you feel now is nothing compared with trying to answer the question, "Am I bisexual?" when the feelings of a wife and children have to be taken into consideration.

Many families react negatively when they find out their children are bisexual or gay. But blood ties are difficult to break completely. As time passes and they see that their "different" children are leading happy and productive lives, parents tend to reconnect with their offspring and show acceptance. I can't promise that your family will eventually get over whatever antigay feelings they have, but keep it in mind as a possibility. You have a right to be happy, and it's obvious that trying to please them is not working. This is a difficult time, but if you reach out, you will find the help you need.

14}

After many years of denial, I have finally admitted to myself that I'm gay. My problem is my spirituality: I was raised in a conservative religious family (Baptist) that looked down on homosexuality as sinful. Now I'm having a difficult time reconciling my belief in God and faith in the church with the knowledge that I am exactly what I used to condemn. I don't want to give up my faith (I haven't yet come out to my family or my church), but I'm not sure I can have it both ways. Are there other denominations that interpret the Bible differently or are any more tolerant of people like me?

There are indeed. It's not necessary to abandon your faith entirely just because you're gay. There are many other ways to worship that are better suited to someone like yourself than taking Communion with a bunch of judgmental fundamentalists who interpret the Bible as the literal word of God (a Bible that, as a matter of historical fact, has been passed down, translated, retranslated, added to, deleted from, and had its content otherwise altered for political reasons for hundreds and hundreds of years).

Odds are that the church you were raised with was affiliated with the Southern Baptist Convention, one of the largest—and surely the most conservative—Baptist groups. As recently as 1987 the SBC denounced homosexuality as "a manifestation of a depraved nature" and "a perversion of divine standards." However, even within the Baptist denomination there are other major groups that take less of a hard line toward gays. While the SBC's policy is to refuse membership to individual churches that don't condemn homosexuality, an organization called the American Baptists believes that we're all sinners, so they're open to anyone interested in salvation.

Of course, you're *not* a sinner just for being gay. (My belief, for what it's worth, is that if you're gay, it's because God made you gay, and denying it or trying to change it is, well, opposing God's will.) And there are churches that will tell you that too. The Unitarian Universalist Association is possibly the most gay-friendly denomination; it's been a defender of our kind since a 1970 declaration of gay rights. Today, the Unitarians conduct same-sex–union ceremonies with high spiritual (if not legal) significance.

We've been off the hook with the Society of Friends, better known as the Quakers, even longer: In 1963 they officially asserted that homosexuality is no more of a sin than left-handedness. (Individual congregations, despite this edict, aren't always so open-minded, however. Assess them on a church-by-church basis.) The United Church of Christ was the first Christian denomination to ordain an openly gay minister, and it has issued supportive statements regarding gay civil rights. The Episcopal Church has also been fairly open.

The most virulently antigay brands of faith are Mormon and Seventh-Day Adventist. Methodist, Lutheran, and Presbyterian groups generally span the spectrum, from outright acceptance to rote rejection. The Roman Catholic Church has staked out the peculiar position that homosexual orientation is OK as long as you don't act on it. Once you perform homosexual acts, only then does it becomes a sin.

Among the other major world religions, Judaism—specifically, the Reform brand—has been very open to gays. (Conservative Jews are less accepting; Orthodox Jews, even less so.) Islam officially proscribes homosexuality, but it still happens—wink, wink—fairly commonly. Buddhism is perhaps your best bet if you decide to abandon Christianity entirely; it condemns neither homosexuality per se nor sex between unmarried persons. Actually, this faith has a lot of appeal to it; its emphasis is on achieving enlightenment rather than salvation, and how an individual gets there is really his own journey to make.

Whatever you decide to do, don't let them make you hate yourself. More and more evidence indicates that we're born gay, and once that's demonstrated conclusively, the Jerry Falwells and Pat Robertsons of the world will be left with no convenient scapegoat for society's ills.

15}

The questions I have are probably common, but I would appreciate your advice. I am a 24-year-old virgin. I am very cautious about approaching or getting close to any man because I'm never sure whether he's gay, and I'm too shy and self-conscious to make any inquiries.

I've heard the term "gaydar," and I would like to know how reliable it is. During my last two years of college, I had an experience with a guy who would look at me a certain way and would even sit or walk by wherever I was. I always wondered whether there was anything going on and whether he was gay.

Another question I have is what, if any, sensations are experienced through prostate stimulation? I realize that the only way I'll know is by experiencing it firsthand, but as silly as it sounds, I'm a little scared about my first sexual experience. Please provide some answers and reassurance for a naive gay man.

"Gaydar" is a nice concept; we'd all like to believe that we can pick our own kind out of a crowd. But given that more and more straight men are aping our hairstyles and innate fashion sense these days, it's getting harder all the time to tell the breeders from the queers. You want to make sure before you make a move on the guy who's staring at you from across the room that he wants to bed you and not beat you to a pulp.

In social situations where you're pretty sure that everyone present is gay, you have it easy. Otherwise, there are some quick tricks to scoring a quick trick. Asking your pals if they know the humpy number by the punch bowl is a good way to start. Or, if you're feeling especially brave, drawing him into conversation works even better. While you're talking to him, drop hints about your very gay personality and ask him questions designed to determine which side of the garden he prunes. Maybe mention a dead film actress you're fond of or ask him which clubs he likes to go to. If he mentions a local gay bar, you've hit pay dirt; if he doesn't know who Marlene Dietrich is, you could be out of luck.

Some other clues to look for: Does he live alone? Does he mention a girlfriend? Does he speak warmly of Newt Gingrich? If you're in a hurry, try this: Compliment him on his haircut. If he scowls, he's straight; if he drops a curtsy, he's a big old Mary.

You're not silly to be scared about your first sexual situation. Regardless of what anyone might tell you, we were all a little nervous the first time someone wanted to put themselves up inside us. The best way to find out how it feels to have your prostate stimulated is to do it yourself. Start by putting your finger up there. Use a lot of lube and take it slow. I promise you, by the end of the first week you'll be buying a lot more zucchini from the A&P. And the next time some cute guy is dogging you, you'll have one more reason to follow his lead.

16}

For about three years now, I have been secretly gay and have kept it from my family. I've had girlfriends in the past but never had sex with any of them. I enjoy sex with men, but now I think I'm falling in love with my best female friend. She tells me she doesn't think I'm really gay.

My family hates gays and says that we will all burn in hell. I know what the Bible says about homosexuality, but how can you mask something that makes you who you are? I really don't know what to do, but I do know that I need advice. Should I go ahead and date this girl to see if this just may be a phase I'm going through, or do you think I'm really gay?

You may or may not be bisexual, but you're certainly confused. And it's no wonder, considering the people in your life and their sophomoric, hateful attitudes about homosexuals. If your gal pal is really a friend, she'll lay off the advances and her insistence that you're "not really gay."

How the hell does she know? If she loves you, she'll let you work through your desires and figure out for yourself whether you prefer boys or girls.

It seems pretty likely, given several points you make in your letter, that you're gay and not bisexual. You've never had sex with a woman; you're concerned about what your parents and the Bible have to say about homosexuality; and you tell me in your first sentence that you're gay. If this were just a phase, you'd have made your way through it by now and wouldn't still be questioning your preferences.

Explain to your friends and family that you're exploring your options and advise them that if they're not willing to love you unconditionally, you'll need to distance yourself from them for the time being. It's tough enough becoming who you are without others telling you who they think you should be.

And by the way, the Bible says nothing whatsoever about homosexuality. The word was coined in the 19th century, when a medical term for same-sex attraction was deemed necessary. There are three vague allusions to same-gender sex in the New Testament and six in the Old Testament, but none of these should be used to justify hatred of queers; Jesus never once spoke on the matter. Tell that to the next Bible-thumper who wants to condemn you to hell.

17}

I am an 18-year-old guy from Louisiana. I still live with family and for various complicated reasons will be dependent for at least three more years. I understand that this magazine does not have anything to do with minors, but I need advice for me and one gay friend who is younger than I am. I just want to know what teenagers like us should do. Not being openly gay is the hardest thing, especially for someone our age. I will always have to hide from my family—they are mostly Jehovah's Witnesses. My family is the most important thing to me, and that is something that I don't want taken from me.

I am still in school and live with my aunt because of the poor education in the schools where my parents live. This town is small. No one is openly gay, and not many people are gay-positive. I guess it was an act of God of some sort when I found my special friend. But right now I need a lover, and he is not my type. When I am in school, some of my peers call me names. I guess

they can tell I am gay by the clothes I wear or for some other rea-son that I can't figure out. I don't like going anywhere or doing anything because I know I can't find someone who is like me without it getting back to my family. Please help me.

The Christian right is always objecting about corrupting young people by teaching them about homosexuality in public schools. The fact is, gay and lesbian teens are al-ready in those schools. If more information were available to kids in your situation about gay life and if supportive counseling were available to gay teens and their families, it would drastically reduce the rates of depression, dropouts, addiction, suicide, violence, pregnancy, HIV in-fection, and homelessness among young gay people.

Unfortunately for you, we don't live at the end of the rainbow flag quite yet. Fear of parental disapproval keeps many people from coming out. Only you can decide what is right for you, but hiding who you are is not a recipe for a happy life. I recommend you contact the National Fed-eration of Parents and Friends of Gays, 8020 Eastern Ave. N.W., Washington, DC 20012; (202) 726-3223. Or try the national office of Parents, Families, and Friends of Lesbians and Gays, 1101 14th St. N.W., Suite 1030, Washington, DC 20005; (202) 638-4200.

One of the biggest problems that young gays have is a lack of privacy. If you can rent a post office box or a mail forwarding service, you can hook up with the Lambda Youth Network, P.O. Box 7911, Culver City, CA 90233. The group has a newsletter and a pen pal program. If you can find a private pay telephone, contact the Sexual Minority

Youth Assistance League at (202) 546-5940, ext. 8, or write to 333½ Pennsylvania Ave. S.E., Third Floor, Washington, DC 20003-1148. Its youth help line is available Monday through Friday, 7 p.m. to 10 p.m. Eastern time.

Eventually, you will be able to leave home. Then you will have more freedom to figure out what kind of life you want. In the meantime, you have a difficult task. Keep your head and your spirits up. There is nothing wrong with who you are. The hostile people who ridicule you are the ones who have a problem. Don't isolate yourself any more than you have to—it's depressing. Stay away from drugs and alcohol. They might temporarily make you feel better, but they will make it more difficult for you to make long-range plans and remain in control of your life. Try to finish school. You will find it much easier to take care of yourself if you have a high school education. This awful time won't last forever. I wish there were more I could do to help; your predicament is one of the worst (as well as one of the most common) problems that gay men and lesbians face. But many of us have made it into adulthood, and you can too if you don't let ignorant and bigoted people damage your self-esteem.

18}

My problem is that I am married and have children but have just realized that I'm gay. My wife does not know yet. I realize now that it was a mistake to marry—I thought perhaps I might change, but I now realize that I can't stay in the closet forever. Though I've never had sex with a man, I know for sure that I'm gay and cannot stay married the rest of my life. Which way is better for me—to lose the children and live my life or to live a lie and keep the children? Which way is safer for the children, with me or with their mother?

Congratulations on finally coming to terms with yourself. You are at a very important crossroads in your life.

You owe it to your wife to be honest with her, and you owe it to yourself to be happy. Though you may love your wife and certainly love your children, you will never be truly happy living a lie. I think you know that you need to start over as a proud gay man, and unless your wife is amenable to some sort of open-marriage arrangement, this probably means divorce.

In that case, unless she is an extremely unfit mother, it is likely that your wife will get custody of your children. You should be able to get visitation as long as you're a good father and stay out of legal trouble, but it is unlikely any judge will grant you full custody.

Will your homosexuality adversely affect your children? Far from it—I think it will teach them tolerance and broad-mindedness, qualities that will serve them well later in life. In this way your coming-out may actually be a blessing to your children. Yes, divorce is traumatic, and especially if they're young, your children will have questions that need to be answered. But children can never have too much love, so if you find a good partner who loves them like his own—or if your wife eventually remarries—then they could well benefit from having two sets of loving parents.

19}

I am facing a very difficult problem. I am 40 years old and have been happily married to a woman for almost 11 years. We are totally committed to each other and have always had a full and active sex life. We're both highly sexual individuals, and we had a wonderful and exciting physical relationship—until seven months ago.

Despite my marriage I've always known I was attracted to men. I've been aware of my homosexuality since my teens, though I've never disclosed it to anyone or acted on my feelings with another man. I don't know why; maybe it was just my upbringing or fear of being found out. I dated women off and on, nothing serious—then, at 29, I met my wife, and we were married ten months later. She had no inkling of my homosexuality, and I never told her. For the next ten years, it was wonderful. We did everything a family does.

Then one evening I went out with some friends and got ex-

tremely drunk. I came home, and for some reason I still don't understand, I confessed everything about myself to my wife. Needless to say, she was devastated, and the next day she left me and
moved in with a friend.

A week later she called me and told me that after giving it a lot
of consideration, she wanted to give our marriage another go—
but only with the stipulation that I never tell her any more about
myself. I agreed, and by that evening she was home again.

But now things are not the same anymore. She treats me and
even talks to me like a different person. Sexually, things aren't the
way they used to be either. No longer do I have the urge to jump
her and fuck her like there was no tomorrow. Most of the time I
can't even keep a hard-on long enough to fulfill her, and now I'm
having trouble getting off as well. We no longer talk like we used
to, and she wants no outside help. All of this is taking its toll on
me and our once-happy marriage. I'm ready to say "Fuck it!" and
move on. What do you think?

Things are *not* the same between you and your wife, and
it's doubtful they ever will be again. This is because by
telling her that you're actually gay, you've fundamentally
changed the entire dynamic of the relationship.

Which is not to say that the marriage can't be saved or
that your marital problems are all your fault. You were
merely being honest with your wife and telling her the way
you really feel—that you're attracted to men and always
have been. As a result, however, there are now obstacles

in your relationship that must be dealt with.

You've known about your homosexuality for a long time and have had time to adjust and learn to deal with it, but try to imagine what a bombshell it was for your wife. If her behavior toward you now is different, it's because *you* now are different. You're gay. In the back of her mind, she now has to wonder whether she's making you happy or if you'd really rather be with a man. The poor woman's whole world has been rocked to its very foundations, and I'm sure she's filled with all kinds of doubt.

For your part, it sounds like you long ago reached a peace with your desires for men and were able to control them and maintain a heterosexual facade. But now things have changed, and I suspect your difficulties in performing are related to stress over this turmoil. Where you stand now is at a crossroads: If your wife makes you happy (as I'm sure she does) and satisfies you sexually in a full and complete manner (you'll have to look long and hard inside yourself to answer that one), then your marriage could be worth saving. Unfortunately, it probably can't be done without outside help; a marriage counselor will probably be required to help both of you sort through your confusing emotions.

If, however, after 40 years of life and ten years of marriage, you are still having these strong desires for men, then you may have to admit to yourself that you are indeed gay and that only by coming out and leading your life as a gay man can you be truly happy. It takes a lot of courage to admit this, especially if you've repressed yourself for so long. But there are support groups and other resources out there to help you through it. If you reach this conclusion and decide to act on it, write back; I can provide you with some addresses and phone numbers.

Whatever you do, treat your wife with the respect and dignity she deserves. Do not promise her fidelity and then go out and sleep with other men. (If she agrees to an open relationship, that's another story, but cheating on her isn't the right thing to do.) If you want to stick by her and try to work through this, then give it your best possible effort, and if it works, great; but if it doesn't, have the courage to admit it and make a change then.

No matter what you decide, I promise you that you cannot achieve true happiness by living a lie. You must be true to yourself, whether that involves sleeping with men or sleeping with a wonderful woman and just fantasizing about men. It's never too late to start being you.

chapter 3

looking for sex

20}

Well, it's happened again. I'm waiting for a bus, and this neat-look-ing guy starts giving me the once-over. And then it happens: "Say," he says, "do you know what time it is?" I just know this is a come-on, but the trouble is, I don't know the answer. Besides giv-ing him the time, what can I do or say to show him I'm interested?

Do you mean to tell me that when people have been ask-ing me what time it is all these years, they were really coming on to me? Oh, the times I've missed!

I'll take it for granted that this was indeed a cruise and not just some guy late for an appointment. If you are read-ing your signals correctly, you'll need to employ the fine art of small talk. It's the same thing you would do in a bar or a gym or any other place you meet guys. For example:

"Oh, it's only 9 o'clock—time for another long, boring day of styling people's nasty hair."

"It's 5:15—happy hour down at the Lavender Lizard. Care to join me for a few brewskis?"

"Beats me; this crappy fake Rolex doesn't work worth a damn. Know any good watch-repair places?"

I overstate here for the sake of making a point; you'll probably want to be a tad more subtle. However, you get the idea; weather, movies, local politics—anything is good to get a conversation going. Usually if you give your time-asker a prompt, he'll contribute as well.

You: "It's 8:30 already. That bus runs later every day."

Him: "Tell me about it. I'm going to be late for my ball-room-dancing lessons."

And off you go.

21}

Since I don't know where else to turn, I will ask for your good advice. I am a handsome young man—6 foot 5, 225 pounds, blond, blue-eyed—and a muscular, in-shape bodybuilder who's also well-endowed with a superbig dick and a tight, muscular butt. I am very hot, horny, and boyishly cute. I'm 26 years old but look 21. I don't have any problem finding male (or female) sex partners, but I find it very hard to meet gay men for friendship and serious dating. I want some gay friends, and I want a serious relationship that goes beyond a one-night stand. It seems that gay guys want me only for my muscles and my big, huge, thick cock. They never seem to care about me as a person! All my life I've been getting offers for sex and many one-nighters, but it seems no one wants a serious relationship, really cares about me, or loves me for myself. It seems that all gay guys are dogs!

Many guys envy me because of my blond hair, blue eyes, cute face, huge muscles, and big, thick, long dick. I've dated lots of girls and had steady girlfriends, but they were too clingy and wanted to get married and have kids. I don't want kids; what I want is a relationship with some good-looking guy like me.

I've tried placing ads in magazines and newspapers; every man I met said he was sincere and wanted a relationship, but when we met he just wanted to park somewhere and get off. I've tried bars, restaurants, and gay social groups, and it was the same thing: I find gay men who care only about themselves, and all they want is sex, not a life partner.

I want someone to share my love with without playing games. The gay men I've met seem to be flaky and unreliable. They'll say they're interested in something long-term, but then they never call, and I never see them again.

I'm getting tired of this same old scene. It's so empty and superficial. When I had a knee injury a few months ago, none of the gay men I know even called to see how I was doing! No one called except my straight friends and family. And when I had pneumonia and bronchitis a few years ago, none of my gay friends cared at all about me. They treated me poorly and even called me a mess!

So where can I find a good, caring guy for a long-term relationship—someone handsome, tall, cute, muscular, and blond like me? I've read hundreds of books on the subject, but maybe you can offer some advice. Are all men dogs?

> Gee, I wonder why nobody is interested in your "big, thick, long dick" and all of your other marvelous physical attrib-

utes you go to such great lengths to describe so many times in your letter. Maybe it's because you're coming across as a shallow, conceited, self-centered jerk.

Go back and count in your letter how many references you've made to physical appearances, both your own and those of other guys. It's not other men who are all hung up on appearances; it's you. Unless you can get beyond that, your prospects for a serious relationship are not good.

It may be fun to trick with a guy who's good-looking, but someone who's obsessed with his own beauty will wear really thin really quick. Could this be why guys don't call you back? Not once in your 30-page letter (edited down here for reasons of space) do you mention hobbies, interests, or anything other than your blond hair, blue eyes, cute face, big muscles, and big dick. Do you not have anything else to offer a man? Are your looks and your dick your only redeeming qualities? If so, this is where your problem lies. Physical attributes alone aren't going to cut it.

Long-term relationships are based on more than just looks. Love flourishes when there are common interests, things you can talk about besides "Wow, man, nice pecs." What do you talk about when you're out with other guys? Do you ask them about their jobs, their hobbies, their friends? Do you listen when they talk to you? Do you show a genuine interest in their lives? Would you be open to a partner who's not "handsome, tall, cute, muscular, and blond" like you? There's nothing wrong with wanting to look good and honing your body to peak condition, but if there's nothing of substance underneath that, then no one's going to want more than a one-night stand.

The sense I get from your letter is that the lights are on but nobody's home. Nice staircase but nothing at the top. I don't say this to be mean, but if that's what comes across from your letter, I can only imagine what people who meet you think. You're going to need to make some fundamental changes if you're going to find a man.

Start by developing some hobbies. Read a book. Watch a movie. Go to an art exhibit. Get some interests beyond how buff you can get and how buff other guys are. Then when you meet prospective partners, take an interest in their hobbies, books they've read, movies they've seen. Be an attentive audience. Be genuinely concerned about their problems. It's imperative to be a good listener. Basically, get over yourself and get into others.

Don't go to bars. Keep placing ads. You might join clubs or organizations of gay men. There are no easy solutions, but if you make some radical changes in who you are, you'll be on the right track.

22}

Lately I have developed feelings of attraction for my best friend. He's 19, and I'm 20. My problem is that he leads a straight life, dating girls and even getting serious with some of them. But many of my friends, some of whom know him well, doubt that he is truly straight. I also wonder, but I don't want to accuse him of lying about his sexuality. He's never said he's not gay, but then again, I've never asked. Still, sometimes it seems he may be closeted or in denial.

We've never been overly close, but I can say that he's not homophobic. I don't think he'd be upset if I told him of my feelings for him. Yet that may not get me anywhere but upset and uncomfortable. I do believe he'll get upset if I question his sexuality, because he's known as being straight.

Should I say anything about my new feelings for him, which I am convinced are love? Should I question his sexuality, hope for the best, and go on from there, or should I just keep quiet?

This is a difficult situation to diagnose because you don't say why you suspect your friend might be gay. I'm also not sure just how close you are to him—at one point you call him your best friend, but at another you say you've never been overly close. I'll have to assume that you are close enough to him to make an objective judgment about what his sexual preferences are.

So exactly what makes you think he might be gay? If it's nothing more than idle gossip around town, I wouldn't put too much stock in it; rumors like that frequently don't have a basis in truth. If, however, there are concrete clues more reliable than someone's wagging tongue (does he listen to Barbra Streisand? Accessorize with flair? Vogue his way around the house?), you can make your move with a little more certainty.

Either way, I'm inclined to tell you to go for it. Nothing ventured, nothing gained, as the old axiom says. He might shoot you down, but you'll never know unless you take a stab at it. It's worth finding out.

If he doesn't know you're gay, he needs to know that and have time to let it sink in before anything else. If he doesn't know you're gay, don't spring that and your crush on him at once; that would definitely be too much to deal with. Let him digest these revelations one at a time.

If he already knows you're gay, things get easier. I would approach him in a private, quiet setting. Don't do it in a bar or mall where it's noisy and hard to talk or when there are other people around for whom he might feel it necessary to put up a front. Tell him that over the past few months, you've developed these strong feelings for him that you think are love. Then you can find out if there's a possibility of reciprocation.

Be prepared for any kind of reaction, including outright hostility. It would be a shame for a friendship to end over something like this, but it happens sometimes. Even if he doesn't get mad, he might be straight and uninterested in anything beyond friendship. And even if he is gay, you simply might not be his type.

And if you hit the jackpot and he is gay and interested, then your friendship provides a strong basis for a sensational relationship. Good luck.

23}

I am a confused 21-year-old virgin male. I've never been with another man but would like to. I am a very good-looking, caring, loving, fun, shy, and nice person, but I still haven't come out of the closet. There is a guy who comes into my workplace whom I would love to sleep with, but I don't know how to go about asking him out without blowing my cover. When I ask him if he needs help, he keeps his head down and says no.

I am also afraid of falling in love with the first man I sleep with. What if he doesn't feel the same as I might? What can I do? Please help!

Learning the ins and outs of dating is sort of like learning how to dance. You may stumble a bit at first and even step on a few toes, but with practice you'll find yourself able to do it with grace.

I don't think you should ask out the guy who frequents your workplace. He might be gay, but then again he might not. If he's not, he might take offense at your pass and turn the situation into an uncomfortable one. Why risk potential rejection, especially on your first time at bat? And even if he is gay, it doesn't sound as if he's interested in you. If you had said that he smiles at you a lot or holds your gaze or asks you questions that are sometimes personal, I'd tell you to go for it. But by ignoring your attentions, he's telling you he's not interested, whether consciously or not. Again, why risk rejection? You would be better off concentrating on someone who is as attracted to you as you are to him.

As to falling in love with the first man you sleep with, all I can say is, Don't! Most men who are feeling anxious about their initial encounter want the man whom they first sleep with to be "the one." That way they'll never again have to experience the trauma of the hunt or the fear of rejection. As a result, it is easy for them to place more importance on the relationship than the relationship deserves. This isn't fair to either partner for several reasons.

First of all, you are in a position of self-discovery. You may not be out of the closet physically, but it sounds as if you are emotionally. During the next few years you are going to learn a lot about yourself, about men, and about what you want and need out of a relationship. It is unlikely that you'll be ready to commit to anything serious, since you'll want to experiment more to learn who you are.

Second, because you are so new to the gay scene, your partner will need to assume the role of teacher, not only of sexual techniques but also of social details. He may enjoy this at first, but inevitably things will change. He could start to feel pressured and no longer want to shoulder the burden of teaching you the ropes. It is a responsibility, after all, and that can become a turnoff. He could also begin to feel unchallenged by you, and that leads to boredom. And eventually you will no longer need him to be a mentor. You might begin to resent his advice, and he might resent your resentment. Your relationship will need to be either adjusted or dissolved.

I'm sorry to sound so pessimistic, but first-time sexual experiences seldom lead to love. It is best to be realistic about this to avoid being hurt. Since you are already questioning the feasibility of falling in love too soon, you yourself must be aware of the possibility of this happening. I hope you find an honest, sensitive, and loving partner to initiate you into the gay world, preferably one you know well enough to trust (and one who insists on safe sex). And if he's not the love of your life, don't be discouraged. If you keep your feet on the ground, you'll soon be dancing with the pros!

24}

I'm 18 years old and have recently become openly bisexual. My hormones are raging. I have these urges to grab some of the men at my college and suck them off, but I don't think any of them are into it. I'm from Montana, and I find it very hard to meet any gay or bisexual men here. I've tried the handkerchief-in-the-pocket trick, and nothing's happened. I've been with only one guy so far; we had hot sex for an entire night, and I'm desperately waiting for it to happen again. I'd especially like to have it happen with my ex-change-student friend from Germany—he has the cutest ass on the planet, but I'm afraid to ask if he's interested. He knows I'm bisexual but couldn't care less.

How do I go about letting my friend know I'm interested? If I can't have him, I'd be willing to settle for someone else, but I don't know of any gay hangouts here that I could check out. I'm sorry if this letter seems crazy, but I have no gay friends to discuss this with. Please help!

It's perfectly natural that an 18-year-old who's just beginning to explore his sexuality wants to screw everything in sight. But grabbing your classmates and forcing their dicks into your mouth won't make you any new friends, and it may well land you in the hoosegow.

I recommend steering clear of trysts with your straight school chums. Remember that you have to see them every day on campus, and their embarrassment over what they did "when they were drunk" may lead to unpleasant future encounters.

There are plenty of gay meeting spots in your area where you can hook up with other men who are likely to be more than willing to fulfill your budding fantasies. Try the Lambda Alliance, a campus social and political group that meets weekly on the Montana State University campus. Call them at (406) 994-4551.

There's more information about other groups and hot spots available via MSU's home page at www.montana.edu. Look under "Departments and Centers," then "Student Organizations," and finally "Special Interest." For meeting times and information about upcoming events, try E-mailing the alliance at wwwlambd@gemini.oscs.montana.edu.

And by the way, that hankie trick long ago went the way of pet rocks and platform shoes. The reason you've had no response from anyone is that young queers today don't have any idea what a pink bandanna in your back left jeans pocket means. Use your handkerchiefs to wipe up after your next hot sex adventure, and leave the secret codes to the military.

25}

I work at an automobile plant, and they recently hired this very sexy new guy. They paired him with me to learn the work I do, and now I find it very hard to concentrate with him so close. Everyone at work knows I'm gay, and someone told him this about me. I asked him if it bothered him to work with a gay man, and he told me it didn't, but he did wonder why I never looked him in the eye or spoke much to him. I confessed that it was because I thought he was the sexiest guy I'd ever seen. He told me that he was flattered and that it didn't bother him that I felt this way.

Since then, though, he's been acting peculiar, almost like he's uncomfortable around me. I can't tell if it's because he's nervous about my attraction to him or if it's that he's also attracted to me. He says he's straight and has a girlfriend, but I'm getting mixed signals. What do you think?

Unless your new friend points a grease gun at your ass and smiles, you should probably assume that he means what he says. I have this theory that straight guys don't realize they're flirting with us—even when they very clearly are. I used to have breakfast every Sunday at a little bistro near my home, and the cute guy who waited on me each week always placed his hand on my shoulder while he refilled my coffee cup. He also always winked at me as I was leaving the restaurant. After about four months of this very obvious flirting, I asked him out to lunch. He showed up with his girlfriend and was astonished when I told him that I'm gay.

26}

For seven years I have been gay. Sometimes I lived with my lover, and sometimes we lived apart. For the past two years, we have been apart—until just lately. He went out of state to take care of his mother and came back to me when she died. It just didn't seem to be the same as it used to be. I have been faithful to him except for one time, and that was with a much older lady. We were more friends than sex partners.

I am confused and don't know what to do. I know it is over between my lover and me. There is no feeling or desire to go back to my female friend. I need to know whether I should try to see other men or women. It's been so long since I dated either one. I don't know if I could perform my sexual part with a woman. But I don't know how to go about meeting men. All my friends are straight, and they think I should date women.

I live in a small town. The people who are gay are closeted. The closest bar is 50 miles away. My lover and I always went out of state when we wanted to be around other gay people. They were mainly his friends from before he met me. I have all kinds of gay stuff, including magazines, books, brochures, handcuffs, whips, and more. I could use some of the stuff in a straight life and burn the rest. But I am still not sure that's what I want.

Why not treat yourself to some counseling? It sounds like you could really use a supportive person who would listen to your problems and help you make this major decision. A trained professional could also tell you if you were mildly depressed, which would explain your feelings of ambivalence or paralysis, and help you to get through it. Contact the Kentucky Gay and Lesbian Center, P.O. Box 4264, Louisville, KY 40204, (502) 897-2475 for referrals.

In my opinion, it's much easier to solve the problem of meeting other gay men than it is to solve the problem of not being able to perform in a heterosexual relationship. Fifty miles is not a long way to go to have a social life. And there may be gay bars or organizations closer to where you live. Get a copy of the *Damron Address Book*. Send $13.95 plus $5 shipping and handling to the Damron Co., P.O. Box 422458, San Francisco, CA 94142, or call (800) 462-6654. (In California, add 8.25% sales tax.) Another good guide is the *Gayellow Pages*, published by Renaissance House, P.O. Box 533, Village Station, New York, NY 10014-0533; (212) 674-0120. Call or write for current ordering information.

When a relationship ends, it's natural to want some time alone to grieve and lick your wounds. But don't stay out of the sun too long. Lovers come and go, but life goes on. If you could travel out of state with your lover, you can do so alone. Some of his old friends would probably be very glad to see you. If you want to find a man, you can. People do relocate to go live in cities with bigger gay communities, you know. And if you don't want to move, there are always the personals!

27}

I work in a luxury hotel with many attractive men, including some gorgeous French waiters. A day doesn't go by without homosexual innuendoes and some male-to-male flirting, but I can't tell who is actually gay and who is just joking around. Unfortunately, the guy I am most fond of is one of the most ambiguous, even though he is friendly and even affectionate at times. He can also be obnoxious and uncooperative as a coworker, but that seems to be a French cultural trait. Any ideas on how I can tactfully bring up the subject to him without offending him? If I approach this the wrong way, I can guarantee you that the entire staff will make fun of me in my presence—only in French so that I won't be able to understand them or defend myself.

What a complicated humiliation fantasy you have concocted here. Wouldn't it be much easier just to go to a leather bar and find somebody who would feed you his cock and call you a fag cocksucker slut in English?

Do not cruise boys where you work. There is no safe way to do this. Gay bars were invented so that men could proposition one another without worrying about offending somebody. Classified ads were invented so that respondents could screen for themselves and simply not reply to sexual invitations that do not interest them.

Some straight men are extremely cute and flirtatious. They like receiving sexual attention and flattery from gay men. They may be very willing to have a hopelessly infatuated queer around because they can manipulate, use, and hurt that admirer. Some straight men are even willing to let you blow them if you get them alone, feed them some alcohol, and convince them nobody will ever find out. (And some of those "straight" men are about as straight as we are, but they are never going to admit it.)

There's no way you can bring up the topic of gay sex to this guy without taking the risk that everybody you work with will start treating you badly. Even a low-risk tactic such as asking him what he thinks about current events (such as gays in the military) or a movie (has he seen Torch Song Trilogy?) is not safe because in your workplace everybody hears everything that other people are saying. Unless you think it would be easy to get another job—and you're so hung up on this guy that you don't mind risking unemployment to have a crack at him—my advice is to keep your hands to yourself at work and find another, safer place to cruise.

28}

Recently I was propositioned by a man I'm sort of related to: He's my stepfather's brother. He's 24, and I'm 21. To me he's only a friend, but to the family he's considered an uncle. I'm really in love with this guy, but I'm not sure if I should accept his invitation and get involved with him.

I'm certain that your mother's husband's younger brother is the hottest man in North America. I imagine he drops by the house all the time in tiny, sprayed-on cutoffs and a chambray work shirt with the buttons ripped off. He almost certainly has killer abs and the most remarkably hairy forearms you've ever laid eyes on. I'll bet he finds all kinds of excuses to touch you, and maybe he even winks at you and calls you "sport" when he thinks no one is looking.

Unfortunately, none of this matters. This man is your mother's husband's brother, and you can't have sex with him without disrupting your family life and probably pissing off your mom besides. If you do have sex with your would-be uncle, everyone will find out, and no one will be happy—least of all you.

Think of all the family gatherings that will be ruined by your inability to keep your dick in your pants. Consider the discomfort of having to face your stepfather, who, if he's anything like most straight guys, doesn't like homos to begin with. And think about this: If things don't work out between you and your sort-of uncle, you'll have to see him every Christmas and Thanksgiving anyway.

As you'll discover, one of the nastiest things about being alive is having to remember to think with your head and not your dick. Tell your pal thanks but no thanks, and find a partner you're not related to by marriage.

29}

I realize that when you're young, from your teens through your early 30s, you can have all the sexual experiences you want. But when you hit your 40s, it's all over except for masturbating. I have been trying the phone bulletin boards for about seven years now. Many guys have responded—some from faraway cities, some from my own area. Some have asked me what I look like, and when I told them, they hung up. Some have talked to me for a couple of minutes, then I heard a click as they hung up. Some have said they would be over and then never shown up, while some would show up only to get scared and leave. Others have asked me to come over and then given me the wrong directions or address. When I've connected with men over the phone, they've gotten off before I did and then hung up.

The point I'm getting to is that I'm getting too old for the phone scene. I don't drink, so I don't go to bars. The gay community centers have nothing to offer me, because all of their

programs are held at night, and I work then. Can you suggest a few ideas?

There are actually two issues you bring up that I would like to address. The first is your disturbing statement that "when you hit your 40s, it's all over except for masturbating." Why do you think that rewarding, passionate sexual experiences end just because you turn 40? Men over 40 have just as much to offer a partner as someone in his 20s or 30s and often more—such as self-confidence; a sense of identity and purpose that comes from having lived through a variety of experiences; and the ability to make love in ways that younger men haven't yet discovered because, hopefully, the older men have come to understand that sex isn't just about two gym-perfect bodies getting off.

Unfortunately, our culture (and especially gay culture) holds up the young, perfect body as the sexual ideal. Many gay men feel that if they have a few gray hairs, a less-than-perfect chest, or a few laugh lines, somehow they are no longer attractive sexually or don't deserve to have fulfilling sex lives. Because of this attitude many gay men completely waste their 20s and 30s trying to validate themselves by doing anything to make themselves physically attractive to other men instead of working on their personalities, learning to love themselves for who they are and what they can offer, and learning how to appreciate life and other people. Then, when their carefully constructed beauty starts to fade, they're left with nothing.

By saying that because you're over 40 you can't have

great sex, you're denying yourself what could be some of the best sexual experiences of your life. There are a lot of men both over and under 40 who would love to find someone to share sex—not to mention a relationship—with. Those who don't just don't know what they're missing.

Now that my little diatribe is over, I want to talk about your difficulties meeting people. You say you've been trying the phone lines for seven years without success. It could be you're expecting too much from phone sex. You have to understand that most people who call phone lines are simply looking to get off and get off quickly. Phone sex lines are a place for anonymous, safe fantasy play, not finding love. There's no time to get to know someone. People describe themselves the way they wish to look, not the way they are. Things like love handles and bald spots are magically erased, and the speaker transforms into his or your hottest fantasy for the ten minutes or half hour you're talking. Then, like Cinderella's carriage, he turns back into the pumpkin he is as soon as he comes.

It could be that you're taking it all too seriously. If you don't plan on ever seeing the guys you talk to, have a little fun. Describe yourself as your hottest fantasy and see what happens. Use your imagination and have fun creating scenarios that challenge you and your partner. If the person you're talking to comes before you and hangs up, then just finish the job thinking about what you were doing.

If you're actually looking to meet the guys you encounter on the phone, then of course you have to be honest about what you look like. In that case you have to realize that just like people you meet in person, people you meet over the phone are sometimes going to be scared, nervous, and even creepy. For some guys it's the only way they can connect, because the thought of going out and actually talking to someone face-to-face is too intimidating. So if guys hang up on you or say they'll come over and then don't, it's because they're scared or because the two of you obviously aren't looking for the same things. The ones who give you the wrong directions are just being cowardly and mean.

You also don't have to drink alcohol just because you're in a bar—you can always drink juice or water. You might want to try going out a few times and seeing what happens. But don't just stand around waiting for someone to approach you, because then you will most likely end up disappointed. Talk to people. Even if they show no interest in you sexually, you'll still be learning how to present yourself, and eventually the self-confidence you develop will start to show. Then people will be attracted to you because you present a positive attitude.

Remember that the bar scene is all a big game, and rejection or acceptance is usually arbitrary and based more on lighting and shadows than anything else. Just because someone turns you down doesn't mean you're unattractive, just as someone's picking you up doesn't mean you're such a great catch. Validating yourself on how many people in a bar want to sleep with you is the shallowest kind of self-worth.

If actually going out and meeting people intimidates you too much, you might want to try some of the many computer on-line services available. Most of these services have extensive gay and lesbian offerings, including message boards where you can read and leave messages. I have many friends who have connected with other people who share their interests in this way, and some later began romantic relationships with these people. It's a safe, non-threatening way to find out if someone shares your interests without the pressure of a sexual situation. Then, if you think you might like to meet the person, you can arrange it. There are also boards just for sex, which can be fun too.

Remember that no matter what age you are, you deserve sexual and emotional fulfillment. Don't count yourself out just because you don't look like the boys in the porn magazines. These images are ideals, not reality for most of us, and love and sex come in all shapes and forms. Don't sell yourself short.

30}

After a recent business meeting, I decided to stop at the inter-state rest area in hopes of finding a nice cock to suck. When I got there I was disappointed to find the rest stop busy with vacation travelers. Lines had formed in the men's room of people waiting to piss. I did notice a truck driver, however, who had his hand-kerchief hanging out of his back pocket. Was this a form of gay contact? Could you give me a few signs I could look for on my next trip to the rest area?

Handkerchiefs indeed are frequently used by gay men as a way of signaling other gay men what they're into. The color of the handkerchief represents what the wearer likes, and which pocket it's in tells you whether the wear-er is a top or a bottom. Generally, if the handkerchief is worn on the left, the wearer is active (a top), and if it's on the right, the wearer is passive (a bottom). Keys worn on a chain outside the pocket have also been used to signify the same thing, though this is less common.

While there may be local or international variations, the following color codes should hold true in most places:

Hankie color	What it means
light blue	oral sex
dark blue	anal sex
robin's-egg blue	sixty-nine
white	JO
gray	bondage
black	S/M
teal	cock and/or ball torture
kelly green	hustler
hunter green	daddy
olive, khaki	military
beige	rimming
yellow	water sports
mustard	size queen
fuchsia	spanking
red	fist fucking
dark red	double fisting
light pink	dildos
dark pink	tit torture
burgundy	shaving
purple	piercing
lavender	drag
brown	scat
brown lace	uncut men
brown satin	cut men

These are the most common colors, though there may

be more. A word of caution though: Just because someone has a hankie hanging out of his pocket doesn't necessarily mean he's gay. Hitting on a straight guy with a
runny nose could get the snot beaten out of you.

chapter 4

doing it

31}

Maybe I am oversexed, but I do not consider that a problem. What I like to do is to suck a nice dick for long periods of time, and I find that it is more fun to suck an average-size dick than a large one. I cover my teeth with my lips so that I will not hurt my partner. My problem is that my lips begin to hurt after long periods of sucking. Some others do not seem to cover their teeth with their lips, and I wonder how they keep from hurting their partners. In porn films the actors don't seem to cover their teeth with their lips either. I am into oral sex only, and I would like to learn how I can do it better.

Men with average-size dicks applaud your generosity and practicality! To keep them clapping, here are a couple of pointers: If your lips get tired while you're sucking his hog, you may be sucking too hard. Give your mouth and your partner's dick a rest while you run your lips and tongue over his balls or the shaft of his cock. This will add to his pleasure as well, since continuous sucking can desensitize even the biggest, hardest dick. You can give your lower lip a break by covering your bottom teeth with your tongue for several minutes at a time. Try sucking in your cheeks and dropping your lower jaw while you're blowing him—this will envelop his dick in wet warmth and have him screaming for more.

There are two surefire ways to make sure you're the best cocksucker in town: Ask your partners how you're doing and find out what they like best—they'll appreciate your interest. And that old adage about practice making perfect couldn't be better applied than to oral sex.

32}

I am a 20-year-old Thai man who just graduated from college. I have had intercourse with a few men, but I am still naive about many gay issues: what precautions to take, practicing safe sex, and things like that. The most serious question I would like to ask you is: How do I prepare before having sex with a man? I mean, do I have to clean the inside of my ass before I start to make love? If I have to do so, what is the safest way to do it? And is it necessary to clean the inside of my ass every time I defecate? Please help!

Welcome to the big gay world. If you're going to be fucked, it is definitely recommended to clean yourself out before going bottoms up. Not doing so can ruin the mood quicker than anything for most guys.

Fortunately, it is not difficult to do this. You can flush yourself out with a douche—that is, an enema—purchased at your local drugstore. Just excuse yourself and go to the bathroom a bit beforehand and follow the simple instructions on the package. It's quick and easy and painless and prevents any embarrassment later in the evening. And re-member: *Always* make him wear a condom.

If you aren't going to be fucked but your partner likes to eat your ass, then a shower (with thorough scrubbing thereabouts) should get you sufficiently clean.

33}

I'm a 27-year-old gay Hispanic male. I love to eat ass. Is this a bad fetish or a very good fetish? I've been doing this (rimming) for about 1½ years.

If the man you are rimming is clean and healthy, you won't get sick. The problem is that many guys who look just fine are carrying parasites, bacteria, or viruses that can make you really sick. Eating somebody's ass can expose you to intestinal parasites, hepatitis, and HIV. So it's not something I recommend you do without a latex or plastic barrier. You can make a thin, stretchy barrier for rimming by cutting up a condom. Some people also use a piece of plastic wrap. We know that the latex from which condoms are made will keep viruses from passing through, but similar research has not been done on plastic wrap. Put a little water-based lubricant on his butt, slap the barrier on it, and go. Just be sure you completely cover the area where your mouth is! When you are done, throw the barrier away. Don't use it again; it might have holes in it, or you might accidentally lick the side that was up against your partner's body. ·

34}

Safe sex is very important to me, and I practice it as much as I can. Nonetheless, I love rimming, and when I'm with a partner (I am not presently involved with any one person, so I have sex with a lot of different guys), it's an integral part of our fun. I was wondering what you could tell me about dental dams. Do they work? Where can I buy them? What kind should I look for? Any help would be greatly appreciated.

Dental dams, when used for rimming, provide an effective barrier to bacteria that could be transmitted by putting your mouth up someone's butt. Originally conceived as a way to catch debris floating around in your mouth during dental work, they are also used by women to prevent the ingestion of juices when performing cunnilingus. More recently they have been adapted as a safe-sex precaution by gay men who enjoy eating ass.

Latex dams designed for dental work can be bought in larger drugstores, medical-supply stores, and stores that carry adult novelties such as dildos, vibrators, and other sex toys. They are rectangular pieces of latex a few inches square that are stretched tightly across the asshole, allowing the passive partner to experience the motions of the tongue while at the same time shielding the active partner from ingesting anything untoward. They do slightly decrease the sensation in the passive partner, but no more so than do condoms.

These dams come in a variety of thicknesses, and while the thinner versions may allow greater sensitivity, they are also more likely to tear or puncture, thus undermining their very function. Thicker is probably better.

Dams can be made out of simple condoms. First cut the tip off, then the base, and then slit the condom down the side. This will leave you with a rectangular section perfect for your purpose. A caution, though: Use only unlubricated condoms unless you want to ingest something really foul-tasting. Kitchen wrap such as Saran Wrap can also be used, but be sure to avoid microwavable wraps, which contain tiny pores for letting out steam.

35}

I've been in a relationship for three years now, but I feel I haven't put out as much sexual effort as my lover has. He wants to fuck me, but he has a very large penis. I'm afraid that if he penetrates me, he will tear me up inside. I want to please my lover, but my anus is just too small for his penis. What can I do for him?

That you care enough to oblige your lover is good news, though I'm curious how, if anal intercourse is so important to your relationship, you've managed to last three years without engaging in it.

Like your lover's patience, your wee, taut hole can be stretched. I recommend buying dildos in successive sizes and, along with plenty of lube, using them in sex play with your lover. Start out by using the smallest of the dildos and, as you become more comfortable, have him use a larger dildo on you the next time you make love. Eventually introduce his penis into play—and into yourself.

Butt plugs are also effective in enlarging the anus, and

wearing them to work can be like all-day foreplay. Whichever route you take, go slowly, make it sexy, and remember: Never underestimate either the elasticity of the asshole or the importance of learning to relax.

36}

My partner and I have been together for ten years and are in a very loving, committed, and monogamous relationship. I am 34 years old and until recently suffered from chronic hemorrhoids that were very painful and bled regularly during bowel movements. Both my doctor and I felt it best to have them removed, and I underwent surgery about three months ago. After the operation the surgeon told me that mine was one of the worst cases he had ever seen.

Recovery has been slow and uncomfortable, but I feel relatively back to normal now—except for my sex life. Prior to the operation my lover and I had enjoyed anal intercourse. It was an extremely enjoyable part of our sex life, and it was something that made us feel both physically and emotionally closer to each other. Unfortunately, when we try to make love this way now, it is quite painful for me to accept my lover's penis. It just feels like my rectum is much smaller and tighter. It's frustrating to have had

this taken away from us, as it was our favorite sexual act.

I don't feel comfortable talking about this side effect of the surgery with my doctor. I don't believe he is gay, and even if he were, I'd just be too embarrassed to bring it up. Are there stretching exercises I can try using a dildo? Is there other follow-up surgery that could help this?

I'd like a free blow job and a box full of paste jewels for each time I've said this one: Your doctor *does not care* about your private life. He has heard and seen everything, including the red and bleeding walls of your rectum. Do you really think he hasn't figured out how they got that way?

You are the only one concerned with what your doctor thinks about your sex life. He's not interested in what or who you put up inside yourself. You're doing yourself a disservice by not talking to him about the medical treatments he provides. And you're not getting your money's worth.

Of course, I'd probably be out of a job if everyone felt comfortable talking to their physicians about every little thing, so maybe I should quit my kvetching. But remember: You're shoveling your hard-earned dough over to this guy, so why not ask him to divulge some of what he learned in med school?

You can take heart; it won't always be so painful to take it up the ass. As the muscles and nerves in your rectum continue to heal, your ability to perform your favorite sex act will return. Stretching out your asshole with a dildo will only prolong the healing process, so for the time being you'll need to use your ass mostly for sitting and eliminating waste. And even if there were an operation to speed up the healing process, it would only extend your period of convalescence. Be patient and consider this: You have the benefit of a loving partner to help you through this very trying time. You could do a lot worse.

37}

My boyfriend, whom I love very much and wouldn't change for the world, is extremely overweight. He is about 5 foot 8 and weighs in excess of 300 pounds, while I am 5 foot 9 and weigh about 160. Neither one of us is hung up on his weight (despite occasional hurtful remarks from people we meet), and we enjoy a wonderful, loving, fulfilling relationship.

Our problem is in the bedroom. Because of his size, we have not attempted anal sex, which I enjoy very much. We have not been able to find comfortable positions, and when we do find one we think will work, he has trouble staying in it for very long, so we can't finish the act. I have been unable to find any books or resources dealing with this subject. Do you have any suggestions as to how we might be able to fuck?

What a great letter to get. So many guys can't look beyond another man's exterior, and that's a shame. We've been so conditioned as a society to abhor obesity that many kind, intelligent, worthwhile individuals have difficulty finding partners due solely to their size. For you to look past your boyfriend's ample exterior and love the man underneath shows real depth and security on your part. It's reassuring to see that there are guys like you still out there.

Having a big partner doesn't necessarily mean a heavy burden on your sex life; you'll just have to be creative in finding ways to fuck. You don't mention which one of you normally tops, so I'll offer suggestions for both partners.

First of all if you're the top: Contrary even to many medical opinions, the missionary position is not an impossibility for you. Your partner should lie on his back with one or two pillows stacked under his buttocks to elevate his pelvis to where you can penetrate him. Varying the number or size of pillows will change the angle of your penetration, thus providing both of you with different sensations. Either of you can hold his legs up.

If you can bear your partner's weight on top of you, the traditional female-dominant position is even better, as it facilitates contact with other erogenous zones like the chest and nipples. Lie on your back and let him straddle you. Of course, in this manner you don't have control over how his weight is distributed, so if it becomes uncomfortable, you'll have to switch. If you find his stomach getting in the way, he can always rotate so his back's to you.

Doggy-style has long been considered the best way to penetrate a well-fed partner. Those who have studied the subject say that the size of the bottom's thighs and buttocks does not seem to affect either partner's pleasure; as long as you can get it in him, this is probably the best way to go. A variation of this is for him to lie on his side and lift one leg and for you to straddle his lower leg and insert yourself sideways.

If you're the bottom, many of the same positions will still work. If your partner tops you missionary-style, using the pillows under you will make it easier for him to penetrate. Don't be afraid to help guide him in, as his visibility may be limited. Having him on his back with you straddling him is easier still. Doggy-style penetration might not work if he tops you, as his stomach could get in the way, but the sideways method will still work if you flip around like you would to sixty-nine, then just align your genitals.

If your partner encounters shortness of breath and stamina problems, try the stop-and-start method used by men who battle premature ejaculation. He can rest up during short breaks, and you both can prolong your fun.

If none of these suggestions work, dildos can be used to simulate penetration and fill that gaping hole. You are limited only by your imaginations.

chapter 5

std's and safer sex

38}

I'm a 30-year-old closeted gay male, and I live with my mother in a small Southern town. I had my first sexual experience at age 20, but I've been celibate for the past seven months. I've been wrestling with the idea of getting tested for HIV. I know I should, as should anyone who's ever had unsafe sex, but I still have a lot of questions. For one thing, how reliable are home test kits? Also, what are the current findings on whether kissing is safe? What if someone comes in your mouth but you don't swallow?

I've become a basket case mulling these questions over and over in my mind. I carry a thermometer around and take my own temperature at least ten times a day. I weigh myself constantly and obsess over every little mole, freckle, and blemish. I guess if anything good has come from this, it's that I have resolved that I will never again, under any circumstances, have unsafe sex. But in the meantime I'm walking around with this huge burden on my shoulders.

The biggest thing that keeps me from going ahead and getting tested is the "what if" scenario. I don't know what I'd do if I tested positive. I'd be kicked out of my home and disowned by my family and friends, and I wouldn't be able to afford the medicines and treatments I'd need. I have no savings and almost no money. Please advise me on what to do here. I need to put this behind me if I'm ever to move on with my life, but I don't know how.

By the way, I feel great and seem outwardly healthy. I gave up smoking six weeks ago and have gained five pounds. I'm just paranoid about the whole AIDS thing.

One last question: Should the result be negative if and when I do get tested, should I be retested in the future? I've heard that sometimes you have to get tested twice within six months before you can really be 100% sure.

Even today, these are good and pertinent questions, and the answers, hopefully, will be of value to other readers as well as yourself.

By all means get tested. Knowledge can't hurt you, but HIV can, especially if you don't know you have it. The likelihood is that you're worried over nothing, but you need to know for sure. Don't waste your time with the home tests, though, especially if you share your home with a bigoted mother. These home tests are a valuable resource for people in certain circumstances, but given your overwhelming concern with all aspects of your health, I recommend a complete physical. Your degree of worry indicates that perhaps a past partner with whom you played unsafely has since tested positive. A thorough checkup should put your mind at ease about your bloodstream and everything else.

Free and confidential testing should be available nearby if not in your town. Call Alabama's AIDS hot line at (205) 978-7066 for suggestions. The Gay and Lesbian Information Line in Birmingham, (205) 326-8600, may also be able to refer you.

If you're exposed to HIV, antibodies to the virus should show up in your bloodstream within six months. Therefore, if you have been *completely* celibate for seven months, one test should be sufficient. If, however, it's been less than six months since your last unsafe encounter, you should be retested at least six months after that date.

FYI, there is no record of HIV's ever being transmitted through kissing, but wet, sloppy, openmouthed face sucking is regarded as somewhat of a risk just because of the theoretical possibility of blood being in saliva. Letting someone come in your mouth, even if you don't swallow, is foolish. Semen can contain HIV, and small cuts in your mouth that may not even be visible (for instance, abrasions from brushing your teeth) can allow it into your bloodstream. Spunk in the mouth is a big no-no.

Congratulations on giving up smoking and on your newfound commitment to playing it safe. You have made two wise choices that should lengthen your life by many years.

39}

A statement made in one of your recent columns concerns me. I'm a bisexual married guy who enjoys a massage every couple of weeks, and I have a gay masseur I visit regularly. Besides giving a fantastic massage, he enjoys rimming me and giving me blow jobs. I have been seeing this guy for the past three years without much concern for safe sex since I've always been the passive partner and have never sucked him. Should I be concerned about contracting HIV by receiving oral sex?

Also, I've noticed that most models in magazines and videos these days have shaved or trimmed ball sacs and pubic areas. My masseur keeps me trimmed very short there as well, but I always thought it was just for his pleasure. Is it the fad now for the younger generation to shave or trim these parts of their bodies? I have noticed the same thing on many guys at my health club. What are your thoughts? Does shaving reduce the growth of body hair?

Well, first things first. Theoretically, it is *possible* to contract HIV by receiving oral sex. However, it is not, at this point, thought to be *probable*. In fact, it is thought to be rather unlikely. But because it cannot be entirely ruled out, you should be aware of the possibility before determining what level of risk you are willing to accept.

How does one get exposed to HIV by receiving a blow job? Well, HIV is present in the blood of infected people. Say your masseur is infected. Say he has gingivitis or bites his tongue or even scrapes his gums while brushing his teeth the morning before he sees you. Then maybe there's blood in his mouth. Now, say you rubbed a little raw spot on your dick while jerking off last night, or maybe you caught yourself in your zipper or something. Then maybe you have an open cut on your dick. And the infected blood from his mouth can come in direct contact with your open wound, thus exposing you to his HIV. It's not impossible. In fact, it's likely that there are tiny cuts or scrapes or openings in the skin that you may not even be able to see.

Still, all of life is a risk, and some risks are less risky than others. Getting an unprotected blow job isn't as dangerous as giving one, and giving an unprotected blow job, unless you swallow the come, isn't as dangerous as being fucked without protection. My best advice to you is to get all the information you can and make informed decisions as to which risks you are and aren't willing to take.

As for your second question, I don't know who started it or why, but for some reason some important person in the porn industry felt it necessary to shave down models, and everyone else decided to follow suit. For a while it was standard operating procedure for everyone. Sure, there are guys who like the smooth, shaved look (and the bristly, stubbly look that inevitably follows), but there are also many guys who like the hairy, natural look. For some reason their desires were pretty much ignored for a long time.

Shaved or trimmed pubes or balls are easier to care for and may appear neater on camera, but they come at the expense of one of man's greatest and most versatile natural ornaments. From what I hear from our readers, more seem to like hair than don't. Whichever you prefer, you should make your voice heard to magazine publishers and those who produce porno films.

Things could be changing. Lately it seems that hair is making a comeback in both print and video, and *Unzipped* (and its sister publications, *Men* and *Freshmen*) is striving to show guys as guys were meant to be; that is, show the smooth guys smooth and the hairy guys hairy. You'll never please everybody, but variety is the spice.

And no, shaving doesn't reduce the growth of hair. Quite the opposite: It increases it, making it come in thicker and heavier.

40}

Other than a little oral action and some mutual masturbation, I have never had sex with another man. However, at age 33, I know I'm gay, and the desire is definitely there. I wonder if there's a term for what I think I have: a fear of sex. Not the act per se as much as what the other person may have—herpes, HIV, or who knows what else. I see so many guys my age dying; can I ever expect this phobia to go away?

Here's a second question: I also have a huge fetish for going to the dentist. You know, the comfortable vinyl chair, the sterile smell, the white uniforms, the feeling of someone hovering over you while you're in a helpless position. I always have a hard-on during my dental visits. Am I weird?

Second things first: There's nothing wrong with your dental fetish. In fact, your provocative description made me want to run out and get drilled right this minute. It all seems very harmless, and seeing your dentist regularly should actually provide you the additional benefit of a lovely smile. So eat those sweets and remember to never, ever floss.

As for your first question, gay sex is more than simply anal intercourse. Blow jobs and mutual masturbation do constitute varieties of sex, and some guys go their entire lives without ever once having anal intercourse. That's unusual, but it's OK; some guys just aren't comfortable with it, be it from fear of disease or inability to reconcile the erotic and excretory functions of the human posterior. No one says you have to fuck butt to be queer.

Still, condoms do make anal sex relatively safe, so if fear of disease is the only thing holding you back, you should make an effort to get over it. Like a lot of things, it seems scary if you've never done it. But once you get that first time or two under your belt, it becomes much easier, and then you'll wonder what took you so long. Maybe you could get some information before trying it or even talk to someone at your local gay and lesbian community center, but in the end it will be up to you. Find yourself a willing partner, grit your teeth, and take the plunge. You'll be glad you did.

41}

A week or so ago I brought home this guy I'd just met in a bar, and we had wonderful, passionate sex all night (and well into the next morning). We sucked and fucked and did pretty much everything else you can think of. Now, however, I'm noticing a lot of itching in my pubic area. Since I'd just met this guy that night and haven't seen him again since, I don't really know a whole lot about him, but I'm wondering if it's possible that he transmitted something to me. What do you think? I really don't want to go to my doctor about this because he'll just give me the safe-sex sermon again. Please hurry your response; the itching is driving me nuts!

I think it's not only possible but also downright probable that your one-night stand left you with a nasty souvenir to remember him by. But since I can't diagnose you by mail, you do need to get your hardheaded self to the doctor as soon as possible and find out if it's something serious.

From your description of your itching, two possible afflictions come to mind: scabies (mites) or crabs (pubic lice). Both of these are highly contagious via skin-to-skin contact. Both are treatable, though, so don't delay.

Scabies are caused by the itch mite *Sarcoptes scabiei*. Pregnant females burrow under your skin and lay eggs, which then hatch, and the larvae cause fierce itching. If you have scabies, these burrows should be visible as short, thin, wavy lines in your groin area and possibly elsewhere. If you can't restrain yourself from scratching, these can develop into larger lesions that can make you simply want to die from discomfort. Your physician can prescribe a cream that will clear it right up, though, and recurrence and the need for re-treatment are rare.

Crabs, *Phthirus pubis*, are merely pubic versions of the lice that can flourish on an unclean scalp. They can be transmitted during sex and also by shared items like dildos and vibrators. While they're usually limited to the genital area, they can spread elsewhere if you're especially hairy. Crabs can be identified by small grayish white eggs attached to your pubic hairs at the base and by small, dark specks (lice shit) on your underwear where it is in contact with the afflicted area. Treatment is normally a prescribed cream, though shaving of the area may be required. Re-treatment is usually necessary with all forms of lice. Also, wash all your underclothes and bed linens thoroughly.

Both of these scourges can be transmitted even if you're using a condom, so don't worry about your doctor's safe-sex lectures. If you're still not playing safely by this point, there's nothing any of us can do for you.

42}

I fear I may have developed anal warts. In recent weeks several small bumps have appeared around my anus—not on the cheeks but circling my asshole. They look pretty much like regular warts you might get on your hand or someplace else. They're not causing any pain, and I've been told they're not dangerous, but I definitely want them removed. What options do I have?

Well, the first thing you should do is visit a doctor. Maybe your diagnosis is correct, but if it's not, you definitely want to find out—and the sooner, the better.

Genital warts—or *condyloma acuminatum*—are caused by a virus transmitted through skin-to-skin contact. (There is no practical difference, aside from the location, between genital and anal warts.) The incubation period—the time between transmission and the exhibition of symptoms—is normally up to six months but can be longer. The lesions appear as pink or brown cauliflowerlike raised areas on the skin or even sometimes inside the rectum or the urethra.

Possible treatment methods include the application of acid to burn off the warts; freezing them off; cautery (electrical destruction); or laser vaporization. Unusually resistant cases sometimes require the injection of interferon, a naturally occurring substance manufactured by white blood cells, into the warts.

Because anal warts are caused by a virus, they are, unfortunately, incurable and could recur throughout your life. Regular visits to the dermatologist can remove them, though, and they pose no serious health hazards. They are also extremely contagious and easy to spread to partners, so, top or bottom, *always* use a condom.

43}

Not too long ago I met a gorgeous guy, and we went out on a few dates. He has everything I've been looking for in a man, and I have found myself quickly falling for him. However, there are a few problems. First, he doesn't seem to have much time to spend with me, though he has plenty of time for his friends. Also, it seems he has a drinking problem, and when he's had a few, he gets awfully flirtatious with other guys at the club. Plus, he lies a lot about little things, things that aren't really worth it.

I want to be with this guy, but it seems like an awful lot to put up with, and that's not even all of it. On two occasions he has tried to have unsafe sex with me, and that really concerns me. The first time I blamed it on the beers he'd had, but the second time he wasn't drunk at all. Does he not know anything about AIDS? I wonder now if he practices unsafe sex with all of his other partners. He seems intelligent, but the way he's acting makes me wonder. He just doesn't seem to care, which makes me

suspect that he's already infected (though I hope I'm wrong). When I try to talk to him about it, he gets upset. What can I do, Tony? I really like this guy, and I don't want to lose him.

Let's see—your man is unavailable to you, possibly alcoholic, a liar, unfaithful, and plays dangerous games with both his life and your own. If this is everything you've been looking for in a man, friend, you are setting your sights much too low.

While I'm sure the sex between you has been good, physical attraction alone is not enough to sustain a serious relationship, and in your case it sounds as though he doesn't view this relationship quite as seriously as you do. After all, you do say he's still seeing other men. And if he flirts with other guys in your presence, tipsy or not, he doesn't value your little affair as much as you do. Prepare yourself for the realization that while he may be your everything, to him you're probably nothing more than a nice, casual way to get his rocks off.

What's more serious yet is his refusal to practice safe sex. This is not a game; this is a life-or-death issue. You are obviously aware of the dangers his practices pose, and by the lengthy discussion of it in your letter (parts of which were edited out here for reasons of space), I can tell it concerns you very much. Unfortunately, besides making him aware of the facts about HIV and of your reservations about his recklessness, there's nothing more you can do. He's an adult, and if he is determined to behave stupidly, then it's his choice, not yours. You can't make him put the love glove on when he's with someone else.

You need to have a long, serious heart-to-heart talk with him, and the sooner, the better. He needs to be aware of your concerns if he's not already. Your top priority must be to protect yourself, and that means no unsafe sex with him *ever*, no matter how angry or upset he gets. Beyond that, it also means that if he insists on having unsafe sex with others, you should probably stop seeing him. If he has HIV or AIDS, it doesn't necessarily mean you'll get it, but you'll have to be very careful. And if he is infected and is spreading the virus through unsafe sex with others, knowingly or not, he is potentially a murderer. Do you want as your partner someone with that little conscience or remorse? (Knowing you're HIV-positive and having unsafe sex with someone without telling that person is actually a crime in many places, and he could face prosecution if such a law exists in your state.) And if he doesn't have HIV, drunken unsafe sex with a lot of men he barely knows is a good way to get it.

If he disregards your very legitimate concerns, he is not worth your time. Say "*Sayonara*, baby," and don't delay. You deserve better.

44}

I am facing a difficult problem with my feelings toward a man I once loved. He is now 34 years old and a long-distance truck driver; I am 24 and used to be a trucker myself. We fell in love back in Wisconsin when I was 20 and had just gotten out of the military. We had a lot in common, holding many of the same values and ideas. We moved around and worked together, and we had the normal ups and downs you'd expect in the course of a relationship. We split briefly a few times but always ended up back together.

Late in 1994 he told me he was HIV-positive. Needless to say, I was scared because I had cheated on him a few times. There was a brief period when communication between us was at a standstill. Then I suffered a head injury in a truck accident. I was hospitalized for five weeks and still suffer some memory loss. But all the way through this ordeal, I remembered that I loved this man. He even took unpaid time off from his job to stay at the hospital and help me through the physical and emotional pain I was in.

But, as they say, all good things must end, and a month after I got out of the hospital, he changed, becoming someone I didn't like very much. He became quiet, closed, and uptight, and we finally stopped seeing each other.

We've been apart for a year now, but every time I'm with him for more than a few hours, I fall back in love with him as if nothing had ever changed. And he says he still loves me and hopes we can someday be a couple again. He is the first and only man I've ever dated or loved, and since he is friends with my mother, I still see him occasionally.

A small side note is that I am still HIV-negative after undergoing five blood tests in the past year. I have tried going out and meeting other people, but I am very uncomfortable going where other gay people are. I also feel that somehow I am the one who gave him HIV, since he tells me that I am the only one he's ever had sex with, protected or otherwise. I would like to either get over him on a permanent basis or get back together with him. But the harder I try to get him out of my mind, the stronger my feelings for him become. Am I dumb for letting this man go?

First things first: If you are HIV-negative, then it is not possible that your ex-lover caught HIV from you. If you have been exposed to HIV, antibodies should show up in your bloodstream within six months. If you have been tested regularly for a year and have done nothing in that time to expose yourself to the virus, then it is almost certain that you are not infected. Unless your ex contracted the virus through a blood transfusion or intravenous drug use, he is lying to you about never having been with anyone else. There are no two ways about it; you can't catch HIV from someone who doesn't have it.

Your other questions are more difficult to answer. I cannot really judge, based only on your letter, whether you have a future with this man. If he still cares about you, as he says, then he should be honest about his other partners. More important, if he wants to get back together, what is he waiting for? Unless there's a good reason for delaying, he may just be stringing you along.

Also, what exactly is it that you want? It seems that you want the old lover you once had, not the new person he became after your accident. Has he explained this change in behavior to you? Is he still "quiet, closed, and uptight"? If so, then he is someone you yourself say you "don't like very much," and he's certainly not someone you want to date.

If this man refuses to explain or address your concerns about his behavior, then you should probably try to get over him and get on with your life. If you still have feelings for him, then you should not see him again under any circumstances, not even socially. That's just subjecting yourself to pain you don't need.

chapter 6

coming

45}

I'm a 43-year-old circumcised man who's never leaked a drop of precome in my life. Since most men seem to produce at least some of this stuff—actually, I've never been with someone who hasn't; I seem to be the only one—I'm wondering whether there's something wrong with me. I asked my doctor about it, but he just shrugged his shoulders, and none of the books I've read seem to cover this topic.

Don't get me wrong; I'm glad I don't flow like a faucet like some guys do, but a little lubrication would be nice now and then—especially when I'm playing with my Prince Albert ring or beating my meat.

I eat a well-balanced diet and take vitamins and minerals by the handful every day. I have at least one orgasm a day (usually self-induced) and often have two, three, or more. I have no problem getting an erection, but my erections have never been "as stiff as a board," if you know what I mean. My penis is not large;

it's about 5½ inches long when completely erect. I wear boxer shorts and have since I was a teenager. Any thoughts?

Tickling a trickle from your Cowper's glands isn't as simple as taking the right vitamins or wearing the proper undergarments. Less than 1% of ejaculate is produced by the testicles, so it doesn't matter whether you're dressing them in boxers or lace panties—your balls have little say in the matter.

The major source of ejaculate is a pair of little charmers called seminal vesicles, which are pouches tucked behind the bladder and the prostate. Most of the rest of what dribbles from your dick is manufactured by your prostate, and the remainder is produced by those charming low-hangers as well as those two pea-size glands mentioned earlier—the Cowper's glands, named for the nice man who first discovered them.

Your Cowper's glands produce the sticky stuff we call precome. For most men, precome drips from the urethra during sexual arousal and before ejaculation. But your inability to manufacture this natural lubricant is all genetic and is no reflection on your manhood. You may be the sexiest stud in the stable, able to launch hot loads across the room, but if you can't dribble a little before you shoot, it's in your genes. There is nothing that can be done about it.

Relax. Who needs it? It isn't safe to use the stuff as a lubricant (precome usually contains live sperm and is just as likely as semen to carry HIV), and, given its potential dangers, precome can get in the way of a nice, long blow job. So add "no dripping" to your sexual résumé and make the most of being dry.

46}

I have a problem: I come too fast. No matter how hard I try to hold off, I always seem to shoot before I'm ready. This is true whether I'm being sucked off or fucking my partner, and it's really a problem. What can I do to last longer? Are there exercises I can do or medication I can take?

My secret for prolonging foreplay always elicits shouts of horror from the men I've shared it with, but here goes: When I feel myself getting close to orgasm, I think of my mother. It works every time.

If conjuring up Mom's face is too distasteful, there are other options. Lasting longer means more intense orgasms, which is reason enough to learn to slow yourself up. Try this little exercise the next time you're home alone: Masturbate very slowly until you're just about to come, then stop and breathe deeply for about 15 or 20 seconds. Do this three or four times; then the fourth time bring yourself to orgasm. The next time you masturbate, wait until the fifth time before you come. Add another pause each time you masturbate until you're able to stop and start a dozen times before coming.

What you're doing here is teaching yourself to break your reflexive over-response to genital stimulation. Once you've gotten this new rhythm down, you'll be able to apply it in the company of your partner. If he's in the habit of playing with your cock the whole time the two of you are getting it on, move his hand away from your dick and to other parts of your body.

If this doesn't work, close your eyes and pretend he's Ellen Corby.

47}

I am a 21-year-old man who has been sexually active with men for many years. All the men I have been with have always been really nice and understanding about a certain problem that I have, but it bothers me nonetheless. I have been with a lot of different men and have had a couple of relationships that lasted for quite some time. But no matter how much I am attracted to whatever man I am with at any given time, I always have trouble reaching orgasm with him, and most of the time I do not.

The thing that bothers me about this is that I have been masturbating since I was 14 and have no problem when I am by myself. I have tried several different techniques recommended by friends, but they have rarely worked. I have tried abstinence for a week or more to make myself horny, but that only makes it worse when I don't reach orgasm. The only times that I have been able to have an orgasm with another man were when I masturbated myself to that point.

When I am having sex, I feel like I am not able to concentrate enough to really enjoy it. Many times stray thoughts—such as what I have to do at work the next day—slip into my head, and by the time I've chased them out of my head and have gotten back to thinking about sex, I'm not excited enough to reach orgasm. Sometimes I get so close that I just know I am going to ejaculate, and I concentrate really hard, and the next thing I know, I'm losing my erection. It's as if my erection "thinks" I have reached orgasm when I have not.

When I masturbate with someone else and ejaculate into their mouth, it is the best feeling ever. But when they try to suck me off, it just doesn't work. Are some guys just not meant to reach orgasm by way of being sucked off, or am I just not concentrating enough (or too much) to reach orgasm?

There are dozens of tried-and-true exercises for retraining your mind—and your limp dick—to respond to another man's touch. As with any sexual dysfunction, however, it's wise to look into what's behind the physical problem. You may have some subconscious issues related to losing control or castration, for example, that could manifest themselves in other, more serious ways down the road.

Meanwhile, try this two-handed trick: While you're having sex with your partner, stimulate yourself to the point of orgasm. Then place his hand over yours while you stroke yourself. This will lay the foundation for connecting your orgasm with another man's touch. The first time you do this exercise, go ahead and bring yourself off with his hand over yours. Next time alternate between your hand and his hand on your cock. Eventually your partner should be able to take over and make you come without assistance.

Since by now you have most likely developed the additional problem of preferring your own hand to your partner's, it wouldn't hurt to tell him how you do and don't like to have your dick handled. And unless he's your lover or a more-than-occasional sex partner, there's no need for you to explain your orgasm-in-training. Most men are used to hearing from their playmates what turns them on and what they like to do. In any case, concentrating on not losing your erection is the best way to ensure that you will. Try fantasizing while he's playing with your dick or focusing on a particular part of his body that turns you on. If your mind is wandering, refocus or switch to another position and start again. He'll probably just think you're being versatile.

But no matter what you do—yoga, relaxation exercises, sex therapy—you've got to abandon coming in another man's mouth. You can overcome limp-dick syndrome, but thus far there's no conquering the AIDS virus.

48}

Chest hair: I'm a great admirer of it, just like the guy who wrote in one of your recent columns that he wanted more of it. Working on New York City's Christopher Street, I see all types of guys during the summer, but whenever I spot one wearing a tank top that shows some fur on his chest (a little or a lot is great), my knees go weak.

Every once in a while, when I'm jerking off to images of these hairy men, some of my come comes out (if you'll pardon the expression) solid, like a tiny white worm. I worry that there could be a medical reason for this, but I'm not comfortable going to my doctor about it. Should I be concerned, or does this just happen sometimes?

Apparently it does happen sometimes, since it's happening to you. Your extra-chunky ejaculate is a result of the mix of ingredients in your seminal fluid and has, of course, absolutely nothing to do with your fetish for fur.

When you come you are actually shooting a load of different fluids that combine as they're blasted out of your penis. The various secretions that make up come are not intermixed but are emitted in a fixed sequence. Most of this stuff is semen, which comes from the seminal vesicles. Some of the fluid originates in the ampulla (which joins the seminal vesicles to the prostate) and contains fatty particles known as lipids as well as a lot of other stuff with long names like glycogen, acid phosphatase, and alkaline phosphatase. These lipids are what you're identifying as "little worms." They're merely coagulated portions of your ejaculate that help transport spermatozoa in their journey toward baby making.

It sounds as if you are occasionally ejaculating more of this stuff than spermatozoa or other seminal plasmas. This is no big deal, because the mix isn't as important as the ingredients, and unless you're planning to impregnate someone, the ratio of this to that doesn't much matter.

The only real drawback to coming in clumps is that it's harder to clean off of hairy chests.

49}

Yesterday I was witness to something that piqued my curiosity. My husband of 13 years and I were messing around in the kitchen while preparing dinner, and he blew a load of come like I had never seen before. Two solid streams flew more than 7½ feet (I had to measure because I was so impressed) and would have gone farther if the stove and cabinets hadn't been in their path.

What exactly controls this function and the ability to fly so far? It couldn't be from saving up his jizz, because he had already shot two loads earlier that day with far less projection. Could standing (as opposed to lying down) contribute to this phenomenon? Could the cock rings he regularly wears have played a part?

Consider it a compliment; it's all about you. As far as we know now, there doesn't seem to be any medical reason that accounts for the distance of a man's ejaculation. The most important factor appears to be psychological—that is, how aroused he is. If your lover's fire-hose fountains drench the far wall, then all it means is that he's very turned on by you (and after 13 years, you frisky devil).

Ejaculation is controlled primarily by a muscle called the bulbocavernosus and secondarily by a muscle called the ischiocavernosus. It is purely under the control of the autonomic nervous system, with muscle contractions occurring every 0.8 seconds during orgasm. A cock ring should have no effect on distance; if anything, it could be inhibiting. Nor does the size of the prostate, the position of the body, the size of the penis, or the diameter of the urethra have any bearing.

Theoretically, if a man consciously developed his cavernosus muscles more than the next guy or if he were simply blessed genetically with stronger muscles, his ejaculation distance could be greater. This explains why repeated ejaculations over a prolonged period of time grow increasingly shorter in distance: The muscles become fatigued. Conversely, someone who has gone several days without shooting might shoot farther because his muscles are rested.

Anyone interested in increasing their shooting range can perform what are called Kegel exercises. This is done by contracting the muscles of the pelvic floor—the same muscles you use to stop urinating in midstream. Don't do it while you're urinating, though; try it while driving or sitting in your office. Strengthening these muscles enhances bladder control and is recommended for people with leaky bladders, such as older women who have weakened their pelvic-floor muscles by having many children.

Larger cities frequently have JO or orgy clubs that may or may not have competitions in this field. Such groups are usually very secretive, though, and you normally have to be invited to join. If you should get into one, be sure to invite your Sex Adviser along (strictly for scientific purposes, of course).

chapter 7

relationships

50}

I am a nice, caring, affectionate, 22-year-old Hispanic guy. I'm a little overweight, but people tell me I look great if I dress properly (which I always do). I live in New York City and go to bars frequently, but I still can't find that right guy with whom I can settle down or even form a friendship. I'm a very understanding person when it comes to dating. Do you have any solutions or advice that could help me find my dream lover in this big city?

You have to get out of the bars and start looking in more positive places. Bars traditionally have been places where people meet because they are in some ways safe places. You know that everyone there is gay. You know that everyone there is at least open to the possibility of sex. You may know many of the people in the bar. And if you're drinking, there's the added comfort level of having your nervousness or inhibitions diminished by the effects of alcohol.

However, these very same attributes make bars among

the worst places to meet potential partners. The very nature of bars makes the whole experience a contest right from the beginning. It's all about finding the best-looking guy in the room, about who's going to go home with whom. Most of us get very nervous in bars because we worry about how we appear to others. Our self-worth becomes based on who cruises us or talks to us, and we in turn reject or accept people based on their attractiveness to us. The logic is that if you're a nice guy and you're in a bar, then there must be other nice guys there too. And there probably are. But you probably won't find them because you're too busy worrying about who's looking at you.

A much more positive way to look for a partner is by starting with yourself. If you aren't happy with yourself, then you cannot be happy with another person. Many of us mistakenly believe that if we can only find the right guy to be with, then we'd be totally happy. But it doesn't work like that. Another person cannot take away any problems you might have or make you happy if you are unhappy. That has to come from inside yourself.

If you work on making yourself into the kind of person you would like to meet, you will inevitably find that you attract that kind of person to you. Instead of worrying about whether you're a little overweight, concentrate on doing things you enjoy and that make you happy. Chances are you'll attract a guy who likes you because you radiate a healthy, happy personality.

You live in the biggest, most exciting city in America. There are thousands of classes, groups, and social clubs to join. Find a gay group that meets one of your interests and try it out. See who else goes to it. It may take a few tries to find something you really like, but I bet you'll make new friends and maybe more.

51}

Please help! After a long, frustrating, tiring, and often very discouraging search, I have found Mr. Right. He's not perfect, but he's
perfect for me. He says he feels the same way about me. We met
on a phone line several months ago and haven't been able to get
enough of each other since. We seem to be extremely compatible.

We've confessed our love for each other, but our relationship
is plagued with complications. First, we live about 800 miles
apart. Second, we're both deeply closeted, and for an assortment
of reasons, coming out just isn't a possibility for either of us right
now. Third, for financial reasons he lives with his parents in a
major city where rent is outrageous, so privacy is hard to come
by. Fourth, both of us are finally getting ahead in our careers and
feel it would be foolish to pick up, move, and start over elsewhere, even though it could mean we'd be together.

He and I are similar. I'm in my late 20s, and he's in his early 30s.
Neither of us has had a long-term gay relationship before, and I

**really do love him more than I ever thought I could love a man.
I've considered ending it because of all of the impracticalities,
but I know I could never simply walk away. I have no one to seek
objective advice from. What do I do now?**

Although you may not be able to see them very clearly
right now, you have several options. You can continue to
have a long-distance relationship with this great guy
you've met, but that will mean having a primary love relationship that doesn't include sex. Or you can have a non-
monogamous relationship with him, which would allow
you the freedom to love him while you're enjoying physical relationships with other men.

There's no reason you shouldn't continue to court this
lovely man, but don't lose sight of the very real drawbacks
to long-distance relationships. Besides no sex and huge
phone bills, there's the stunted development that goes
with a long-distance affair. Relationships unfold differently
without daily contact, and phone sex can get pretty tire-
some after a while. Ask yourself how much of what you
feel for him has to do with how long you've waited to meet
someone worthwhile. If you continue to devote yourself to
this relationship, will your long-distance lover eventually
join you in a more up-close-and-personal situation?

The key to a successful long-distance, long-term love
affair is in identifying what your needs are and managing
to get those needs that aren't met by him handled in a way
that's acceptable to your faraway lover.

52}

After coming out just a few years ago, I am now involved in my first real gay relationship. I have dated a few other men and had sex with one other guy, but this relationship is the first one to really turn into something. We have been an item for about nine months now. We have many things in common, and he is a truly wonderful guy, and I think I love him. The problem is that the sex isn't as good as it could be, and the reason is me.

I was very attracted to him when we first started dating, but now he just doesn't turn me on the way he used to, and I have a hard time getting revved up. His appearance hasn't changed or anything like that, so I don't know just what the reason is. I don't know if I'm just getting a little too accustomed to him, so to speak, or if everything was so new to me when I came out that I was attracted to the novelty more than the person. I am constantly lusting over other guys, and it's not fair to him, and it's not satisfying to me.

Unfortunately, he is beginning to realize that I am not enjoying sex with him as much as I used to, and he is trying harder and harder to please me. I can tell it's bothering him. I try to act like I am really enjoying it, but sadly, I am not.

What can I do? I'd hate to give up a great relationship with a wonderful guy over something so shallow. I know I am still young and inexperienced, and that doesn't help. Part of me wants to go out and sample what the world has to offer, and another part knows I've got it good and doesn't want to blow it. Can you offer any advice?

Now is as good a time as any to recall that "I Think I Love You" is a song by the Partridge Family and not a reason to continue a relationship. You are doing both yourself and your boyfriend a disservice by not ending things now, before anyone's feelings get smashed to smithereens.

There could be any number of reasons why you're no longer attracted to the former man of your dreams, not the least of which is that, as you say, you haven't yet played the big gay field. Particularly at your young age, knowing that this is the only guy you'll be having sex with forever and ever would make any man's dick shrivel to nothing.

Whatever the reason, there's no excuse for staying in a relationship that's unfulfilling. The longer you stay, the longer you're keeping both of you from having real, rewarding romances with men you're better suited for. Part of the dating process is determining whether the great guy you've just met is actually boyfriend material. Most of the time the answer is no, though occasionally we are fortunate enough to have bagged a nice guy who will become a friend—like the guy you've been boffing for most of the past year. If half of what you say about him is true, you've met a really swell man who, once he forgives you for misleading him for a little while, will make a great friend. So for both of your sakes, do the deed now and get on with your life—and let him get on with his.

53}

At 48 years old, I am still single. I have a friend who is married but secretly gay. We decided one night to have sex, and we fell in love that same night. His marriage, he says, was over as of that night. He tells me that all the time.

His wife and kids eventually found out about us and gave him all sorts of grief. We parted company, but a few weeks later we were back together. Nine years and hundreds of breakups later, I'm still waiting. I know that on some level we love each other, but he is still in the closet and won't ever come out. Yet when I break it off, he begs me to take him back until I give in and do it. I love him, and I'm weak.

I hate this life and get more withdrawn and depressed each year. I know this relationship will never become the mutually caring union I want it to be. I've tried meeting other guys, but I'm old, and the men out there carry too much baggage. Help!

It seems to me that being a luggage rack would be preferable to being a doormat, which is what you've become in the (mind-boggling!) nine years since you fell under this charming man's spell.

You have two choices, as I see it: You can continue to be weak and miserable and not have what you want, or you can stand up for yourself, brush yourself and your ex-boyfriend off, and get the hell on with your life.

Feeling sorry for yourself and denouncing the entire gay male population of the world won't do you any good. The best place to start is by rejecting the idea that no one wants you because you're no longer 27. There are plenty of pleasant young queers who want an older daddy to tuck them in every night, and surprisingly few of these come with wives and children and the inability to be happily homosexual.

Your present lover is never going to leave his wife, nor will he one day wake up and realize that your devotion deserves to be rewarded. He doesn't appreciate you and has his own reasons for not wanting to make a commitment to his true sexuality. Leave him to these things and take your own life out into the world where it belongs. With a little effort (try the classified "romance" ads and a couple of gay social groups), you'll eventually meet someone who can return the kind of affection and stability it sounds like you are able to provide another man.

54}

My lover and I have been together for about seven months. He is 18, and I am 23. We have been living with each other for four months. Before we moved in together, things were great. Now it's turned into a living hell. He says I'm not to have any friends and can't talk to anyone except my family. I can't even go out to the bars unless he's with me.

The other problem is that he's been talking with his ex-girlfriend and has told her that we need a roommate to help pay the bills. He wants her to move in. This girl is still in love with him, or so she told me (she hasn't told him). It hurts like hell to hear her say that. He has told me that he doesn't want anything to do with her except as friends, but I don't know what to do anymore. I need help.

This is one of my least favorite letters to get. Unfortunately, it's also one of the most common. This is not at all an unusual situation, and there are a lot of men (and women) who have been through what you're going through.

There are a couple of problems here. The most important is your lover's behavior, particularly the way he wants to control your life. It sounds as though this is his first serious relationship. People in these situations often become very possessive and jealous because they are afraid of losing their lover to someone else. They think that they will somehow prevent anything bad from happening by limiting whom their lover speaks to or has contact with. Sometimes this problem can be dealt with by talking about the insecurities each person has and by reassuring the nervous partner that you aren't going anywhere.

Unfortunately, I think your lover is doing this for another reason. While some 18-year-olds are capable of having fulfilling adult relationships, I don't think this man is one of them. He's very young, and it sounds as if he just doesn't know how to behave in a mature, grown-up fashion. If this is his first gay relationship, he probably has not really dealt with his feelings about coming out yet. Until he does he's not going to be a good partner for anyone.

My primary concern is for you. You probably feel on some level that you can help this man or teach him how to be in a relationship. Maybe you even think you can help him come out and accept himself. Well, you can't. No matter how much you love him, he has to do that on his own. And the fact that his former girlfriend is still in the picture just complicates everything even more. If she moves in with you, you'll have twice as many headaches as before, regardless of what your boyfriend thinks.

No one wants to hear this advice, but here goes: You have to get out of this situation, and that means leaving this man completely—or, at the very least, moving out and trying to work out your problems without the added pressure of living together. This is not just a phase he's going through, and it's not going to get better on its own, whether or not the ex-girlfriend moves in. It's impossible to develop a satisfying relationship when you're in such turmoil, and your boyfriend needs to grow up a bit before he even thinks about having a partner. What he is doing to you is abusive. There may not be any bruises or cuts on you, but his behavior is just as damaging to you as physical abuse. If you can, I strongly suggest going to a gay and lesbian community center and speaking to a counselor about your situation. It can really help to talk to someone who's not immediately connected to the problem.

If your boyfriend really cares about you, he will understand why you can't live with him the way he is and he'll be willing to work on his problems before continuing the relationship. If he doesn't understand, if he says you're abandoning him or hurting him, then he's thinking only of himself. Don't let him make you feel guilty; you've done what you can for him, and you have to move on. While ending a relationship—even an abusive one—can be very painful, you have to take care of yourself first. If he's really worth it, he'll get his act together. If he's not, he'll just have to find someone else he can hurt. You deserve better than that.

55}

My mate of 14 years is Hispanic, and he exhibits a lot of the machismo that so many Latin men do. We sometimes pick up a trick when we go to the gay clubs on Saturday nights. This person is inevitably young, very skinny, and effeminate. All these guys want to do once they're in bed is throw up their legs in the air and get fucked. I like to do more. I thought the purpose of a three-way was for all participants to enjoy one another, but all these tricks want is to be used. My lover is happy with this arrangement because all he wants to do is fuck.

I know you will tell me that we have to compromise and that we should look for his type one night and mine the next. Wrong! If I get near anyone that I'm attracted to at the bar and start a conversation, my lover rushes me away, gets mad, or says the potential partner is ugly. We never agree. It's his type or nothing. I usually just give in and let him do the choosing. He will never do the same unless the person I pick is his type anyway.

I love my partner very much, but I am not attracted to these young, effeminate fuck machines. I like man-to-man sex. You might think that I myself am the same type of young, skinny guy

I describe, or else my lover and I wouldn't be together. Well, I was young when we started out, but people change over time. Both of us work out at the gym a lot, and I think he feels I am a threat to his masculinity because of my physique.

In addition to this problem, my lover also has this idea that as long as we are doing the fucking, we have no risk of contracting HIV and don't need to wear condoms. Although I have not been fucked in several years, it still scares me. We are both HIV-negative.

You've done a great job of communicating to me what is troubling you about your relationship. You have clearly thought about it a lot and come to some conclusions. The problem is that you can't communicate in the same way with your lover.

Your lover chooses effeminate men for your encounters because that's what he is attracted to sexually most likely, not because he is threatened by these men. You don't say whether you and your lover still have sex with each other, but you do say you haven't been fucked in years, which suggests that perhaps your lover is threatened in some way by your changing physique and looks to these other men to satisfy his need to be the aggressive, controlling top.

If the men you take home enjoy this—and you aren't threatened by his having sex with others—then that's fine. But you deserve to have what you want too, and you aren't getting it. If you aren't getting what you want sexually from your partner and he prevents you from being with men who might give it to you while insisting that his own needs be met, he is being very selfish.

You have been with your lover for 14 years, so there is obviously something that is keeping you two together. Now that a problem has arisen, you need to sit down with him and tell him that you have needs that just aren't being met. Giving in to your lover on this issue time and time again is eventually going to result in the buildup of a lot of resentment and anger on your part, and while ignoring the problem might seem easier right now, it will just cause more problems later and make you miserable.

Explain to your lover why you aren't satisfied with this kind of sex and why you'd like to try different things. He may just be afraid that you'll find someone you prefer over him, in which case you'll need to spend a lot of time reassuring him that that won't happen. If he still insists on always doing things his way, then he is just a self-centered and controlling person, and you will have to decide whether this is a relationship you want to remain in. Your happiness and emotional satisfaction are much more important than where he shoots his load, and if he is so selfish and insecure that he can't make compromises for the man he supposedly loves, then perhaps you're better off without him.

As for the issue of HIV, your lover is making what could be a deadly mistake. HIV is transmitted when there are openings in the skin that allow it to enter a person's bloodstream. If your penis has any cuts or scratches on it, it is possible for the virus to infect you through those cuts. Anal sex can often cause the receptive person's rectum to bleed, and even though you don't see any blood, it doesn't mean your penis isn't coming into contact with infected bodily fluids. HIV needs only a microscopic cut to pass into your bloodstream, so any unprotected anal sex is dangerous, even for the top.

56}

My partner of seven years has recently admitted to having had five or six flings over the course of our relationship. I've never been unfaithful—until recently. I've been in severe lust with a straight coworker I'll call Dan. I've fantasized about Dan since I was transferred here several months ago. I've never hidden being gay, nor have I flaunted it. One day after work Dan and I went out for a few beers. He asked me that night if I was straight or gay. I admitted that I was gay, and that was the end of it. More beers. Eventually we ended up at his apartment (Dan doesn't have a car, so I drove him home). We started watching a straight porn movie, and Dan asked me if I was getting aroused. Of course I was—by the proximity of him! He claimed he wasn't, and he put my hand on his crotch to prove it. I was in shock, but I didn't remove my hand. I continued to feel him up and eventually undressed him. My mouth explored every inch of his body that night, from his neck down to his ankles. I understood and respected his wish not to kiss. He beat me off to orgasm, but I could not do the same to him. We had both had a lot to drink, and I blame the beers.

I'm being transferred again in a few weeks (still in the same city). All I can do, however, is think of Dan. He's a great guy, not to mention hot. Would I do him again? Yes! Now what do I do?

I suppose a great deal will depend on how Dan reacts during your next encounter. By the time this is published, you will have seen him at work. At that point he will have either renounced his heterosexuality, thrown himself into your arms, and begged you to leave your lover for him; thanked you for a fun evening but warned you that it can never happen again; or pretended that the whole thing never took place.

If you brought Dan screaming out of the closet—which I think is unlikely, given the way these things usually unfold—and he has the same feelings for you that you have for him, then you have a decision to make: Leave your cheating lover or try to save a relationship you've invested so much time and heartache in. As that's not really your question, I won't get into that.

So, say Dan is straight and insists on playing it that way. That leaves you with the painful dilemma of unrequited feelings. If you can never have this man, it is pointless to torture yourself. Take your transfer, get on with your life, and try to forget about Dan and your wild night of passion.

Conversely, Dan may acknowledge that he was drunk and horny and open to experimentation but that now his curiosity is fulfilled. He may want to remain friends. Unless you can separate your feelings of friendship for him from your feelings of desire, this will be an exercise in self-immolation for you. Don't torment yourself by pursuing something that's out of reach. Go after what you can get; it's a lot less frustrating.

Dan may also claim that he was too drunk to even remember what happened. This may be true, or it may be just a cover to protect his shaken sense of masculinity. Either way, if he's not willing to face up to it, you can't force him. Don't linger over the situation.

A fourth possibility is that Dan, like many straight (bisexual?) guys, will want to continue to get "a little on the side" while dating various women. Unless you and your lover are both amenable to the possibilities of an "open" relationship, this means potentially throwing over your lover for a regular fuck buddy. In this eventuality you will have to decide whether it's worth it to trade a serious, long-standing relationship for infrequent casual sex. It wouldn't be for me.

The issue beneath the issue here (and maybe the real reason you wrote) seems to be between you and your lover. The way you describe it, your antics with Dan sound like retaliation for your lover's infidelity. You surely were hurt, and quite understandably, by your lover's disloyalty. Now what to do—forgive or be on your way? Only you can decide if the relationship is worth saving. Obviously, there was something strong enough to keep you together for seven years. My advice to you is not to let it go without a fight. If it can't be saved, it can't be saved, but make sure you've exhausted every avenue that might salvage something. Seven years is too much of an investment to walk away out of hurt, anger, or spite.

57}

I was involved with a guy who has always said he is straight. We had a very good sexual relationship even though he was always insisting to me that he is truly heterosexual. But because of our relationship, his family and friends abandoned him, and he eventually committed himself to a mental institution and was treated in an effort to "cure" his homosexuality. Now that he's been released, he has told me that his religious beliefs will no longer allow him to continue our relationship.

This is not the first time he's broken off our relationship for this reason. He tells me now that he loves me as a friend but cannot have sex with me. He says he wants to date women, but so far he hasn't. This breaks my heart because I love the guy. I've accepted it, although it's very confusing to me. He doesn't practice any organized religion but is influenced by Mormon beliefs.

I haven't seen or heard from him in a while, but I don't want to give up on him. I need a way to convince him that there's nothing

wrong with being gay. I did not choose to be homosexual; God made me this way, and I accept it. Can you help us?

The saddest thing in the world is a gay person consumed by so much self-loathing. This is a good time to remind everyone that no religion, therapy, or treatment can truly "cure" homosexuality—they can only make you hate yourself. You are exactly right: If you're gay, it's because God made you that way.

Unfortunately, if your friend was raised by a bigoted religious family and has spent his life surrounded by bigoted religious friends, he's not going to see it this way. He's going to continue to deny himself. There are two possible outcomes to this: 1) He will go to his grave having lived a miserable, deceitful charade of a life; or 2) he will realize later in his life that he's been fooling himself and wasting too many precious years. Neither of these outcomes is very appealing.

Your problem now is that he views you as an enemy. He may profess to love you as a friend, but he also believes that you are a bad influence, someone who wants to lead him astray. For this reason your arguments aren't going to have much impact on him, no matter how rational or persuasive they may be. He's just going to tune you out.

So what can you do? Simply let him know that you're there for him, not as a lover but as a friend who cares about his welfare and as an ear that's willing to listen to what he has to say. His desires for men aren't going to go away, and he may someday wish to discuss them with you. Be a friend and forget about sex for the time being.

Make sure he knows that you support him unconditionally (something his church cronies do not). It's difficult, but
that's all you can do. You can't force him to come to his
senses, but perhaps time will.

58}

Recently I met a young man at a local cruise spot. We hit it off instantly, and now we spend a lot of time together. We plan on moving in together in a few months. I am 36, and he is 20, good-looking, and very sweet and attentive. So what's the problem? Let me begin at the beginning.

I am currently married, but my wife knows about my relationship, and we plan to break up. I have three children: a daughter, 18; and two sons, 11 and 7. My young man, "Brandon," went to school with my daughter and used to spend time cutting class at our house. Now the years have passed, and he means more to me than she does. He tells me he loves me with all his heart.

The problem (maybe it's just my insecurity) is that Brandon has an ex-lover in a neighboring city for whom he cleans house every Sunday. When he goes there it just crushes me. He pages me regularly while he's there, but he doesn't want me to meet this ex—he says it would be awkward, that we have few of the same interests. I tell him it would ease my jealousy if I were to meet him. Brandon usually goes over about 11 a.m. and returns very late or spends the night there. He says I should trust him, that he and his ex are just good friends.

Then one night I went out and happened to see Brandon at another local cruise area. He spotted me immediately, assumed I was checking up on him, and told me he was headed straight home.

Brandon lives with his mother and brother. I've talked to them both by phone, but Brandon says I can never come up to the door and meet them, that I have to pick him up in the driveway. I tell him this makes me feel like he's ashamed of me, but he says his mother has her own problems to deal with and can't deal with this one too. She's unhappy with our age difference, but he says to hell with her on that.

I don't know what to think of this situation or if I have a future with Brandon. I love him, but I feel like I always take a backseat to his ex. He tries to reassure me and gets mad when I get insecure. What do you think?

I think love is blind, brother, and you're a real Ray Charles.

As an impartial observer, I think this boy is playing you for a fool. The Sunday-night sleepovers are reason enough to be suspicious; "housecleanings" generally don't require 24 hours. It certainly is possible to be friendly with an ex, but Brandon's relationship with his is highly suspect in light of his refusal to let you meet this person. OK, maybe they are just good friends, but then why keep you apart? You don't have to socialize, just meet face-to-face once. And you and the ex do have at least one common interest: Brandon.

Catching him at the cruise spot clinches it for me. Someone who's in a steady relationship has no need to frequent such areas. There is no reasonable explanation for his presence there.

There are too many coincidences going on here. People who are up to no good will often try to shift the blame onto their victim, as he is doing by attacking your "insecurity." If you have expressed your discomfort with all these situations to him and he refuses to address your concerns, I think your worst fears are confirmed. In fact, it would not surprise me if Brandon had gone on his merry way by the time this letter sees print.

If it's any consolation, most of us have been used and hurt at one time or another by someone for whom we cared deeply. Love really can blind you to the not-so-pretty reality.

And incidentally, what kind of father lets school-age kids cut class at his house?

59}

My first relationship was very lengthy, lasting almost 20 years. I met him when I was a scared and lonely teenager trying to find out who and what I was. The horrors began about six months after the relationship started. The remaining years were a living hell. My life was filled with devastating verbal and physical abuse, public embarrassment, humiliation, and continuous terror. I was totally controlled and manipulated to the point where making even the smallest decision was not in my best interest. I learned to keep quiet, lie low, and pray like hell that tomorrow would be a better day. My friends would tell me to get out before it was too late.

Well, I finally got the nerve to end the terror and move on with my life. Since the end of that relationship, I've been in therapy and have facilitated a support group for other victims of domestic abuse. It was very rewarding and made me feel that I could help people and hopefully bring closure to that part of my life.

The problem now isn't with the past but with the present. A

year ago I met the man of my dreams. He's wonderful, and I love him to death. I've tried to explain away the past, sometimes with little success. The questions range from "Why did you stay so long?" to "Why didn't you fight back?"

Further complicating my current life is the fact that I now cannot express anger for fear of what might happen. When "John" and I disagree, I clam up and don't utter a word. John tries to figure out what's wrong, but to no avail. I want to be able to express my feelings to him, but I simply can't. Even after all the years of therapy, my brain tells me to communicate, but my heart tells me to be careful. So I remain silent, and the cycle continues.

I'm frustrated because I don't want to lose this wonderful man I've finally found. He's so special to me, but I can't figure out how to help him understand. He's doing better but is still puzzled by the entire situation.

Could you please help me help him understand what I've been through and that it takes time? I'm trying the best I can, but I feel that it's not going quickly enough. I need John to understand before it's too late. He doesn't believe in therapy for himself, so having my therapist explain it to him won't happen. I'm at a loss for ideas. Please help!

First, let me offer you sincere congratulations. It takes a lot of courage to end an abusive relationship, especially one of 20 years' duration. And to turn your negative experiences around and use them to help others is extremely noble.

Recently there has been a renewed national focus on domestic abuse. But the victims of such abuse aren't exclusively heterosexual women. Abuse happens in every demographic group, and that includes both male-to-male and female-to-female abuse in the gay community.

Typically, victims of domestic abuse suffer from low self-esteem, which prevents them from saying "I don't have to take this crap" and walking out. They rationalize their spouse's abusive behavior, telling themselves things like "I deserved it" or "If I just don't provoke him, it'll be OK." Of course they don't deserve it, and the situation almost always deteriorates rather than improves. The longer you wait and the more it happens, the harder it becomes to break the cycle.

People like John, who have never been involved in an abusive relationship, can't be expected to understand what makes people stick around and take it. Nor will they fully appreciate that the aftereffects of such violence can linger for years. Your current lover needs to learn more about domestic abuse and the impact it can have on victims. After 20 years of bottling up your emotions, you can't simply flip a switch and become open and expressive again. As you recognize, it will take years of therapy and unlearning behaviors you've spent so much time learning.

This is why it is important for John to go to therapy with you. Whether he realizes it or not, your inability to communicate is his problem too. Twenty years of oppression cannot be resolved in a quick, convenient fashion. If John really cares for you, this is something he should be willing to do.

You might find some help from the New York City Gay and Lesbian Anti-Violence Project. This group publishes brochures on domestic violence in gay and lesbian relationships. These complimentary brochures are available by writing to 647 Hudson St., New York, N.Y. 10011, or by calling (212) 807-6761. Also, Lambda Project Oasis features trained counselors who can talk with the two of you about this issue and resolving its lingering effects. You can reach them at (718) 447-5454.

60}

Here's a long and sordid story made short: My lover and I became friends with another local gay couple, both very attractive, if a bit shallow. We would go over to their apartment from time to time to watch movies. All four of us would pile onto their queen-size bed (the VCR was in the bedroom) and get under the covers to watch what we had rented.

From almost the very first time we did this, one of these guys started making surreptitious contact with me under the covers. At first it was just his leg brushing against mine, but he would hold it there long enough to raise my suspicions (among other things). I thought it was innocent at first because he was always very vocal about being monogamous with his partner. But then it escalated to hand contact, his hand against my leg or vice versa. When he didn't get the position next to me in the bed, he would force rearrangements until he did. By then I knew the contact was intentional. And, to be honest, because my relationship was about to end, I was interested too. Finally, one night he leaned over to reach for a soda on the nightstand and quite purposefully pressed his erect cock against my thigh. At that point I gave him a good grope through his pants.

Throughout all this nothing was ever said to our respective lovers. But then the sexual tension reached the breaking point, and the couple abruptly and mysteriously cut off all contact with us. Later I found out that this guy had told his lover that I had started all the touchy-feely stuff under the covers and had tried to break up their relationship. A lie, of course, though I will own up to some guilt in flirting.

The postscript is that my relationship was the one that soon ended, while the big flirt and his lover are still together (apparently happily). None of us sees one another anymore, but in hindsight I still have some questions: Did I read the signals wrong? Should I have reacted differently? Was he just jerking me around? Am I wrong to want to chop them up into little pieces and bury them in my backyard?

When someone intentionally presses his erect cock against your leg, that's a hard—er, difficult—signal to misinterpret. But as to whether this guy really wanted to leave his lover for you, well, that's tougher to answer.

I suppose it's possible that he wanted to dump his lover and begin a new life with you. It's also possible that he was simply looking to have an affair. Maybe he just wanted the thrill or the ego satisfaction of some heavy flirtation. Maybe he was trying to instigate a three-way or even a four-way. It's hard to tell from this vantage point. If they're still happily together, maybe there were just some temporary relationship problems that drove him to seek solace in the arms (or legs, as the case may be) of another man.

If you're interested in "should haves," yes, you should have confronted him privately and asked, "What's going on here?" And yes, you have a right to be a little irked about the way it turned out. But that's all water under the bridge now. Learn from it, forget about it, and move on.

61}

This is a real dilemma, and I'm very close to having a nervous breakdown over it. About a year ago I met a gay couple who had been together for almost seven years. About a month ago one of the guys, "Stan," accused me of having sexual feelings for his lover, "Mark." Mark and I are close, and I know that drives Stan bonkers (he can't stand to have Mark out of his sight for more than five minutes), but I don't know where he got this idea that I'm in love with his boyfriend. It's just not true, and it's messing up my friendship with Mark.

To make matters worse, Stan then told my mother that I'm gay and in love with his lover. I've kept my sexuality a secret for 21 years, and then he comes along and blurts it out to her.

I know Mark and Stan cheat on each other. They live with "Jim," Stan's ex-lover, and Stan and Jim got busted by Stan's sister recently—she walked in on them while they were fucking. So if he's doing that, why can't I be friends with his lover?

I'm afraid my friendship with Mark will end because of Stan and his jealousy. Should I fight for my friendship or turn my back and walk away?

Who needs *Melrose Place*? To hell with *Sally Jessy Raphaël!* You probably never even turn your television on anymore.

If you don't need melodramatic TV shows to keep you entertained, then you also don't need a friendship with someone whose lover abuses you. This time Stan outed you to your mother. (A despicable act if there ever was one, but considering what you've told me about him, this sounds like one of his more charming recent endeavors.) Next time it could be something worse. You don't want to be on the other end of Stan's plan to rid the world of everyone his lover has ever had lunch with. Get out now before this wacko really flips his lid.

Tell Mark that while you prize his friendship, you can't risk the pain and discomfort his sick husband is visiting on you. There's no need to take Mark to task for not standing up for you to his lover or for not preventing Stan from outing you to your mom. Mark surely knows his own shortcomings; I'm certain Stan chants them like a mantra every day for everyone to hear.

Walking away from this unfortunate triangle and making friends with some nice, healthy gay men will do wonders for your self-esteem. Volunteer at your local gay community center or join a gay square-dancing troupe. Send Mark a Christmas card every year until he wises up and dumps that awful whore he's living with. Then—and only then—you can investigate the possibility of a friendship with your former pal.

62}

For the past three months, I've been dating a porn star. I'm 18, and he's 22. Now, I know I'm young and stupid, but I really feel like I'm in love with him, and I can't see myself without him. He's done everything in his power to help and protect me, and I'd do anything for him.

When our relationship started he was also dating a woman. Recently he told her that if she didn't give him his space, it would be over between them, so she's given him that space. He told her that he likes the "game"—that if he knows something is his, then he takes it for granted. Then he told me that I should learn from their experience to make sure our relationship lasts.

Can you explain what this means and what options I have? Should I feel so depressed over him?

> Let me give you the no-bullshit translation of what your porn-star paramour told you: I'm going to sleep with other people, so if you want a piece of me, you'd better learn to like it.

No matter how he tries to sugarcoat it, this is what he's saying. You are not going to be the only love interest in his life. You can be a fuck buddy, but you're not his one and only. He's going to play the field, and you're just one part of that field, of that "game."

If you're OK with this, then there's no problem. You can see him at his convenience, but don't bug him when he has other plans. On the other hand, if you're an all-or-nothing kind of guy, then you have a choice to make: Is part of him better than none of him?

My advice is this: If you can handle the situation without jealousy, then go ahead and enjoy it for what it is. If you're even slightly uneasy about it, though, it's probably better to move on. You'll have many other partners in your life, and some of them will even respect you as a lover and a person, not treat you as some disposable plaything who exists primarily to stroke their ego.

63}

After ten-plus years of looking, I finally found the man of my dreams. Tim and I met through the classifieds about two months ago and fell in love (we live in the same town). Having loved and lost, I was afraid of moving too fast, but our relationship took off like greased lightning. Tim wanted me to meet his daughter, and we got along great. Tim then mentioned giving me the keys to his home and having me move in, all in the first week and a half! But as time passed I felt something was amiss, and Tim said three things were wrong.

First, he was afraid of how his being gay and our relationship would affect his daughter. Second, he worried about how his family and friends would react to his being gay. Third, because of me, Tim couldn't work as much as he wanted.

I told Tim I understood and was willing to slow down and give him space. In my opinion, Tim's friends, family, and daughter don't need to know about us until they ask. In the meantime, I can be introduced as his friend or roommate (when and if I move in) should the need arise.

Tim hasn't said it, but he's made me feel like he doesn't want me around his daughter right now. She spends every other week with him, which means we go at least a week without seeing each other. Tim also doesn't have to work as much as he does, but he likes the extra money and wants to pay off his home and car loans early.

In the two months we have been together, we have been out only once. However, Tim and his daughter went out for a "daddy and daughter" weekend, and later I learned his friends were invited to spend the day with them. This weekend Tim took his daughter to see his parents, and in coming weekends he has to cut firewood for the winter on his dad's farm. Being disabled, I can't do much, but I did offer to help load the wood. I thought this was a good way to meet Tim's parents and spend some time with him; Lord knows, loading firewood is not my idea of a good time.

As it stands now, I feel all I am good for is sex. I enjoy making love with Tim, but I am starting to resent this. I want Tim to have a good relationship with his daughter and to be able to work all the overtime he wants, but I also want some time with him. It doesn't help that I am disabled and don't work—I tend to sit by the phone and wait for his call. Am I being unreasonable? This is my third gay relationship and Tim's first, and other than our not having enough time to spend together, Tim is the perfect man.

First of all, you're dealing here with someone who's still in the closet. Tim is not necessarily using you; he probably wants to keep you apart from his friends and family because he is not yet ready to come out to them as being gay. Give him space for this—you can't push him out until he is ready to make the decision on his own.

A week and a half is far too little time to get to know someone before asking him to move in. Perhaps Tim's subsequent recalcitrance is an indication that he realized he was moving too fast. Or the three items he cited as being "wrong" may mean that he is not as serious about the relationship as you are. You need to have a heart-to-heart talk and make certain you are both on the same page.

You do not mention how old Tim's daughter is, but in rural Arkansas she is bound to be exposed to a good degree of homophobia. I would not divulge your relationship to her until she is of at least junior-high age. Children have very concrete concepts of right and wrong, and it could cause her a great deal of confusion if she's too young to comprehend that society is simply incorrect in some of its moral strictures. Her whole faith in what's good and right may be shaken if she's too young to fathom the concept of "live and let live."

Fear of this may play a part in Tim's reluctance to fully commit. He may feel that he has to keep his love and family lives separate in order to ensure the health of both. This could be just a father's protectiveness. Or maybe he just has some emotional baggage of his own to work through, given that this is his first gay relationship. Then again, if one judges by his behavior (weekends without you, lots of time apart), he may be having second thoughts about the entire thing.

This is why I recommend a good face-to-face clearing of the air. Sit down to talk in a collected, unemotional way. Explain your problems and reservations. Tell him you want the honest truth, no matter what it is. You may even show him the letter you wrote me.

Regardless of the result, each of you will at least know where the other stands. It is imperative to be at this point before your relationship can progress. A lifetime together will require complete, unadulterated honesty.

64}

I am 70 years old and have been sexually active with men since I was 22. I have been in a monogamous relationship for more than three years with a much younger man of 37. He has never had a sexual experience with a man other than me. In my head I think he should, but in my heart I am not sure how to handle this. We have talked about it, and he says sex and love are two different things. It's going to happen eventually, I am certain. I sincerely feel that he will stay with me, but I'm not sure how I'll react when he has sex with another man. This is the first time I have gone this long without cheating.

Your beau's desire to explore other sexual avenues could turn out to be beneficial for both of you—and your relationship besides. Since you seem certain that he's eventually going to have sex with another man, now is a good time to review your options.

You say you're certain that he loves you and will stay

with you, and you point out that this relationship marks the longest you've gone without cheating. Surreptitious infidelity won't be necessary if your lover is stepping out with other men, because you'll be free to do the same. If it's worth it to you to have his love and companionship—and if you sincerely feel that he should be having sex with another man—give an open relationship a shot. They work for some people, and as long as you set the ground rules ahead of time, seeing other people may satisfy both of you.

65}

I had never experienced real love until several months ago, when I met a college student in his late 20s. He was very nice, and I thought he was very handsome. We started dating. He was also a Catholic and turned out to have a lot of reservations about being gay. He threatened to become a priest every other week or so, and our sex life was nonexistent—although the priest he went to for confession, a personal friend of mine, told me that my boyfriend told him that our sex life was "hot." Mine was, anyway, because in my frustration I was sleeping with a lot of men behind his back.

Although my boyfriend would kiss me in front of the student union when I'd drop him off there (he was president of the gay organization on campus), he didn't want other students at his school to know he was seeing me. As a result, his peers thought he was single and fixed him up with a young man whom he then started seeing behind my back. He eventually moved in with this

other man. After that relationship ended, my former boyfriend moved in with a new lover.

These days we're spending a lot of time together as friends, but I'm still in love with this guy. He says we're too different to be a couple. What's going on here?

As far as I can tell, what's going on is a lot of nonsense that with a few more costume changes might be mistaken for the plot synopsis of an old Lana Turner movie. In simpler terms, you've done what all of us have done at least once in our lives: You've fallen in love with a flake who doesn't deserve your attention.

This man (and I use that word advisedly) is clearly not capable of making up his mind about what he wants, and you've gotten caught up in his indecisiveness. One minute he wants to be a priest, the next he's in love with you, and shortly thereafter he's telling his classmates he's single and letting them fix him up with someone else. Meantime, you're not getting laid—at least not by the object of your affections—so what's the point?

It might help for you to recall that when you were playing boyfriends with this fellow, he wasn't playing fair. As far as I can tell, you were doing all the giving, and he was running around doing as he pleased. The fact that you had to go elsewhere for sex—the primary reason we couple with other guys in the first place, remember?—should have been your first clue that it was time to move on. I agree with your ex: You're better off letting your relationship with him evolve into a friendship because you're different in a fundamental way that won't lend itself to romance. Specifically, you're a man who knows what he wants, and your pal is not and probably won't ever be.

By the way, what ever happened to professional ethics? Your priest friend should not be repeating what he hears in confession, even if it concerns you. Come to think of it, maybe you should fix him up with your ex. They sound like a perfect match.

66}

I'm a 26-year-old gay male who's in prison. I'm involved with a guy who's just barely 20. We've been together for about two months now, and I've fallen in love with him. He says he loves me too and has never felt this way about anyone else. (He's been married and is now divorcing his wife.)

The thing is, I'm unsure as to whether his feelings are true. He doesn't consider himself gay, though I try to tell him otherwise. I'm actually the first man he's been involved with, but then again, he doesn't look at me as a man. I'm a drag queen, and I often wonder if he's in love with me or the "woman" I impersonate. He never really knew any homosexuals until he was incarcerated. I think he's just now discovering his sexuality, yet I also think he's unsure at the same time. He swears up and down that he wants to stay together after we're released. He gets out about a year and a half before I do, and he's going to be living with an older man in his 40s who's also gay. Deep down this really bothers me, but he claims they're just friends. I can believe this to an extent because he's still searching out his sexuality.

Another thing that bothers me is that he's always talking about women and pussy. If we do, in fact, get together once we're out, I worry that he'll cheat on me or even leave me for a real woman. I can't deal with that; I want to be the only one in his life. I myself am not insecure or uncertain about my sexuality. I've been out of the closet since I was 13 and have been active in the gay community since shortly after that, so I know the ups and downs. But I'm still really in love with this guy and just don't want to get hurt. I think we're good together. I can't turn off my feelings, nor do I want to. I do want him to know that I honestly love him. I just wonder what the future holds for us.

If I could tell you what the future held, I'd demand a heck of a lot more money to be the Sex Adviser. But I can tell you what common sense tells me, which is that you're setting yourself up to be hurt.

I don't doubt your feelings for this man, but remember that you are in a somewhat abnormal situation. It's hard enough to forge a successful relationship on the outside, let alone while you're both imprisoned. (Although if your prison lets you dress in drag, I guess anything's possible.)

That the two of you have come together as sources of strength, support, and sexual relief for each other is great, and you are fortunate to have each other while you pay your debts to society. However, it would be a mistake to assume that the same factors that make a relationship work in prison will make it work on the outside as well.

Just because a man turns to another man for sexual relief in prison doesn't necessarily mean he's gay. He may simply be lonely, horny, or seeking the proverbial "any port in a storm," so you can't read too much into the fact that you've had sex or even become close. You say he still indicates a desire for women and that even in prison he aligns with a man who dresses as a woman. It sounds pessimistic, but once your friend is released, don't be surprised if he goes right back to women and you never hear from him again.

Then again, your friend is very young, and it is possible that he's just now accepting that he's gay. Still, a year and a half is a long time to be abstinent and loyal to an incarcerated mate. If he is living with a gay man, he will probably be meeting lots of other gay men. Will someone who has recently discovered his homosexuality be content to sit alone and masturbate during a time that is his sexual prime, or is he likely to go bounding joyously off to explore everything his new lifestyle has to offer?

I'd have to say that the odds of this man's getting out of prison, deciding he's gay, waiting for you, and settling down are extremely slim. If you get your hopes up, you're probably going to be hurt. Enjoy what you have while you have it, but try to keep your expectations in check. You'd be better off starting clean once you're released with someone who is gay and comfortable with it.

chapter 8

sex drive

67}

Recently I was in the Far East, and while eating at a restaurant there, I noticed an item on the menu that really caught my eye: tiger penis soup. I asked the waiter about it, and he told me that tiger penises are a powerful aphrodisiac. I didn't order it, to my lover's great disappointment (the only tiger's penis I wish to consume is his), but it got me curious. Is what the waiter said true? Can eating such disgusting animal parts really increase your sex drive?

Different cultures have different legends about the sexual powers of different things, and penises figure prominently in a lot of them. It makes sense, I guess—after all, what better body part could you consume to improve the functioning of your own penis? Medically and scientifically, however, I know of no great research done into tiger penises and their effect on human potency. I do know, though, that many more repulsive things have been consumed toward that same end.

In Sheikh Nefzawi's *The Perfumed Garden,* he recommends rubbing your penis with the bile of a jackal or melted-down fat from the hump of a camel. Another topical application is—brace yourself—leeches. You put them in a bottle, which is then buried in a dunghill or other warm, moist environment (dunghills just aren't widely available in the modern urban United States) until the leeches have congealed into one homogenous mass. This, if you're strong enough to bear it, is then used for anointing the penis.

In many Asian cultures, antlers, especially those of reindeer and rhinoceroses, are credited with great powers, as are the fins of sharks, usually prepared as a soup. In Greenland they eat the bill knob of the king eider.

Tiger whiskers are used in Indonesia. Throughout Asia, in fact, tiger parts are known for inspiring virility. Bones, fat, and liver all have their proponents, as do penises.

The consumption of penises, wombs, and testes dates back at least to the ancient Greeks and Romans. The Roman author Apicius provided recipes for stuffed womb of pig and cow, and the Greek physician Hippocrates recommended deer penises, which were endorsed by others well into the 17th century.

Even today in the United States, some people swear by seafood, and not just oysters. Lobster and sole are also purported to possess sexual superpowers, and *chipi-chipi*, a small Venezuelan clam, is said to be the best of all.

The aphrodisiac powers of plants and spices would fill another column entirely, so let's leave it at this: For the most part, the sexual function is in your head. The best turn-on of all is still a loving partner.

68}

We have been going out for about six months now, and although I fought my feelings the whole way, I've fallen head over heels in love with my boyfriend. He tells me that he loves me also. My problem lies with the fact that we never (well, seldom) have sex. The last time was a little more than three months ago. We've talked this over, and his reasons are valid: His last relationship was abusive, he's always been used by the men he's dated, and he's addicted to prescription drugs. He's getting help through counseling after a near-fatal overdose three weeks ago. (He spent a week in intensive care and two days in a rehab clinic, which he left when he encountered severe antigay attitudes among the staff.)

Now he is emotionally and physically exhausted, which I understand completely. But that doesn't totally explain the two months of chastity before that, which he attributes to his addiction (he says he was too preoccupied with getting drugs to worry about having sex). Because of his drug problem, he's lost his house, his car, his job, and his dog, and he's living with his mother until he gets his life in order. This places even more strain on our relationship, as if it needed more.

Now I don't know whether to push the sex issue or wait a while and see what happens. As far as opportunity goes, I have my own apartment (he stays here occasionally), where we can be alone. My friends all tell me to dump him; he and his family say he's lucky to have me behind him right now. All I know is, I don't want to hurt him, but I need sex once in a while. I'd be happy with once every week or two. I need some good advice I can trust.

I think your friend is indeed lucky to have such an understanding man behind him. You have been extremely patient and kind, but you may have to be patient and kind for a while longer.

Don't underestimate the addictive power of prescription drugs. Just because a drug isn't illegal doesn't make it safe. Hard-core addicts crave another fix over anything else, sex included, and pills can be just as addictive as cocaine or amphetamines. While your boyfriend was in the worst throes of his addiction, everything else—you and sex included—came second.

The bad news is that he will always be an addict. But if he is committed to doing so, he can keep his addiction under control. He needs to remain in counseling for this, so *do not* let him quit! Keep looking until you find a qualified treatment option that is free of antigay pressures (he may have to travel to a larger neighboring city). The longer he stays straight, the easier it will be, and his sex drive will likely return once he has his addiction in check.

That said, you may also be a couple with vastly differing sex drives. Some guys simply like it more than others, and that's frequently a contributing factor to many breakups. If this is the case in your situation, the two of you will have to compromise. Determine how often you'd like it and how often he'd like it, then settle somewhere in the middle. Once every week or two doesn't seem like too much to ask, so if he's not willing to do that, you may eventually have to part ways.

69}

My problem started in my mid 30s and has continued through my current age of 42. I cannot maintain a steady, hard erection through sex. I start out well, but after foreplay (which both my partner and I really enjoy), my cock loses some of its stiffness. This isn't really a big deal until he lifts his legs or rolls over and says those two magic words. Then I can't get hard enough to roll on the rubber, let alone penetrate. I'm still very excited, and I can still come, but the situation is frustrating and embarrassing—especially since I am usually the top.

Age may be a factor, but I've been with guys in their 50s and 60s who can get it up and going in a blink. I've wondered if diet or the extra 40 pounds I've put on over the past five years could have an effect. My partner and I are both HIV-negative, so we have tried sex without condoms. We enjoy it more—when I can get it in—but the condom doesn't seem to make a difference. Even when I'm by myself, experimenting with a variety of masturbato-

ry techniques and positions both with and without a condom, I can't get beyond that half-hard state. Fortunately, my guy is very patient. Our sex life has much variety, but this situation bothers me a great deal.

It's always difficult to admit that one has a sexual problem and to look for help. Congratulations on taking this brave step! There are several potential culprits that might be responsible for your problem. Perhaps the extra weight is a factor. Maybe you have circulatory problems. Your sex life may not be matching up with your true desires. (Do you really want to be the top?) You really should be evaluated by a medical specialist who can tell you if any physical problems exist. You might also benefit from treatment by a trained sex therapist. By taking a behavioral approach, a qualified sex therapist can treat most sexual problems in a fairly short amount of time.

The American Association of Sex Educators, Counselors, and Therapists, 435 N. Michigan Ave., Suite 1717, Chicago, IL 60611-4067, (312) 644-0828, publishes a directory of members for $15. Include a self-addressed, large envelope (9- by 12-inch).

The American Board of Sexology, 1929 18th St. N.W., Suite 1166, Washington, D.C. 20009, (202) 462-2122, publishes a registry of diplomates. The ABS can give you the names of sex therapists in your area.

70}

I am a gay American service member currently stationed in Europe. I'm very sexually active, to say the least, because basically anyone with a penis can get laid in Europe. I've found that European gays have a much more casual attitude about sex than Americans. Every town—regardless of its size—has at least one sauna, one disco with a back room, and one cruise park. And the fact that I'm young, athletic, in the military, and (most important) an American makes my opportunities for fast-food sex endless.

Meanwhile, back on base, some of my fellow gay GIs have formed a contingent against me, labeling me everything from "the last slut from hell" to "an unenlightened hick" and "a walking cliché." They tell me that promiscuity is no longer a viable lifestyle. One went so far as to diagnose me as being a sociopath; he says my promiscuity is indicative of deep emotional scars, that my refusal to settle down reflects a serious inferiority complex.

My question is, Why does it have to be all that? Can't it just be

that I really enjoy sex? Hell, I'm young, I have hormones, and European men turn me on. And I always wear a condom. So why should I be expected to feel guilty or enter a 12-step program just because I have a high sex drive?

Your complaints are older than Carol Channing: Gay men have been assaulted with other people's sexual ethics since the beginning of time. Judgments of our erotic endeavors are mired in sex phobia and homophobia and, in the age of AIDS, a very real fear of death. Your comrades are probably responding negatively to your carousing for the usual reasons: They think sex is bad; they think gay sex is bad; they think gay sex in the military is bad; and on and on. Maybe, as our mothers might tell us, they're just jealous. Perhaps your enormous good looks and your openness to your sexuality are bagging you more babes than they're getting.

Or maybe they have a point. You're the only one who really knows whether you're truly obsessed with sex. If you think of nothing other than getting laid and if you spend all your social time seeking out your next sexual conquest, you might be hasty in snubbing that 12-step program. Ask yourself: Are you socializing outside of bars and sex clubs? Are you putting quick sexual encounters in place of more meaningful relationships? If so, you might be avoiding intimacy or choosing sex over other worthwhile experiences that require emotions you're not ready to deal with. But if you're leading a full and varied life that happens to include a lot of sex, then ignore those barracks-bound harpies, keep that condom on, and have as much fun as you want.

71}

I'm a 48-year-old male who has shared a relationship with a wonderful lover for more than 20 years. Our sex life has always been active and fulfilling. Two years ago, because of health circumstances, I had to have my left testicle removed. It was a bizarre, gruesome, and painful experience that kept me in the hospital for more than a month. Recovery was relatively simple, though, and nothing was cancerous.

I have noted, however, that in the two years since the surgery, my sexual appetite has diminished. Could this be a result of the operation? To what extent do the testicles affect sexual urges?

I'm surprised that after such a serious operation you still have so many questions. Did your doctor really not explain these things to you following your surgery? If you're not already seeing an endocrinologist, you should definitely make an appointment to do so—he can answer questions about your body's ongoing adjustment and assist you in becoming more comfortable with your scrotum's new single status.

With half a pair of nuts, it's only natural that you're half as horny as you were before your surgery. Your testicles produce testosterone, a hormone that affects your sex drive as well as secondary sex characteristics such as body hair and the tenor of your voice. You're not manufacturing as much testosterone, so it's no wonder that you'd just as soon fold socks as blow your boyfriend.

An endocrinologist or urologist can check your testosterone levels and, if they're low, prescribe treatment that will help you maintain a hormonal balance. Most doctors recommend testosterone injections, but Testoderm patches, which are worn next to the skin, are also increasingly being used. In either case you should be having your levels checked at least annually to ensure that you're getting what you need.

Your doctor might also suggest a good plastic surgeon who can, if you're interested, implant a prosthetic testicle to even things out nicely. Whether you go this route or not, it's time to find a specialist who will answer your questions and not keep you hanging.

chapter 9

body image

72}

I'm a gay male who has always been attracted to men with hairy chests. I would love to have hair on my chest, but I have none. Is it possible to have a hair weave or some other process done that would appear natural? Are there hairpieces or other options available? I have never seen this discussed or advertised, but I find it hard to believe that it isn't quietly available to actors or other men trying to enhance their masculine appeal. I have been too shy to contact businesses that advertise hair-replacement services for burn victims, chemotherapy patients, and the like. But women seek breast enlargements, and I see no difference between this and a man's seeking body hair to enhance his appearance. Do you know of any such businesses, procedures, or options?

How delightful to hear from someone who actually thinks of chest hair as something other than a curse. I've been waiting for the trend in smooth, hairless chests to end and for gay men to come to their senses and stop shearing away what may well be one of the few things that are masculine about them. (Your adviser is convinced that if it became fashionable to have no ears, gay men would line up around the block to have theirs lopped off.)

Unfortunately, it's not as easy or as inexpensive to transplant hair as it is to remove it. Although hair-replacement specialists promise us that hair can be successfully grafted onto any part of our bodies, the disadvantages of transplantation can be pretty hairy. For one, follicles retain the characteristics of their donor site, so hair moved from your scalp to your chest requires frequent trims, and fur moved from your armpits will give you a nice fuzzy chest that might just smell like a sewer.

Hair transplantation works, but it's costly, and the procedure hurts like hell. You can get in line for newly fuzzy pecs by calling the New Hair Institute at (800) 639-4247.

A temporary option is crepe hair (the same stuff that fake mustaches and beards are made of) adhered to your tits with spirit gum. If you go with this suggestion, you'll want to make sure your next paramour keeps his hands to himself—or you may find yourself reenacting that scene from *Valley of the Dolls* where Patty Duke flushes Susan Hayward's wig down the can.

73}

I'm a gay male with a problem that some might call vanity, though it doesn't feel like vanity. Whenever new friends see old pictures of me, they invariably gasp with disbelief and tell me how handsome I was then. It seems that at the age of 54, because of some weight gain, thinning hair, and shifting contours, my physical appearance has changed beyond recognition. Friends who haven't seen me in years say the same thing, sometimes adding how heartbreaking aging can be. I find these statements more painful and depressing than I can tell you.

I never had much awareness of my outside self except through other people's eyes. I didn't even realize how fat I was in high school until kids began to refer to it all the time. Later, as a young adult, I lost the weight and blossomed. But I still had no self-confidence. During my early 20s I went to New York to pursue a career and by accident became a model. I made a decent living in that field for nearly 12 years. Although it had its perks, I considered modeling as little more than a financial stepping-stone toward my career, a career that floundered for years and then failed because of my lack of self-esteem. I came from a strict religious family and grew up "secretly" gay in a small Midwestern town at a time when *queer* was synonymous with *evil* and *freak.*

My modeling days were the pinnacle of my life, which has been going downhill ever since. I've become more and more depressed lately knowing that my basically unsuccessful life is nearly over. Despite a college education (which was incomplete), I have only a poverty-level job and little expectation of finding a better one because of my fear of my own incompetence. Seven years ago my longtime lover died of AIDS. A new one isn't likely because I'm sexually impotent. My good looks, which lasted for only a brief period of time and had nothing to do with me in the first place, probably became a crutch for me, bringing me financial support, lovers, and attention. Now I'm trying to figure out how to get out of this slump.

Barring a heart attack or suicide, at age 54 your life is far from over. You can expect to live another 20 or 30 years at least. Our view of the human life span comes from a time when people had much shorter life expectancies. We think in terms of growing up, getting an education, getting married, and then dying. But many people find that the latter third of their life brings them a new primary relationship and a new career, even additional educational opportunities. Please stop digging your own grave—that's somebody else's job.

It's never too late to change. You have a good analysis of why your life has gone wrong and why you feel so unhappy. But you are too paralyzed by depression to figure out what to do about it. I can think of many options: finishing college, finding a new lover, going to the gym, getting some vocational counseling to see what you'd need to do to get a better job, and finding some new friends who don't say catty things about the way you look. But I think you need some encouragement to take action.

San Francisco has tons of mental-health resources for gay people. Find yourself a decent therapist and get some help. San Francisco Sex Information, at (415) 989-7374, can provide a good list of referrals. You can also call Operation Concern at (415) 626-7000. If you are willing to go to the East Bay, there's also the Pacific Center: (510) 841-6224.

74}

At age 32 it isn't easy to still be in the closet to your parents. I am receiving monetary assistance from them while I finish my college degree, but I plan to come out once I finish my education. To make things even more complicated, I have met a man I really enjoy spending time with. I know he is gay, and he knows I am too. However, I haven't told him that I think I am falling head over heels for him. He is my age, kind, understanding, and a good listener. He has a wonderful personality and is very much a looker.

Here is my problem: I am overweight as a result of a back injury suffered in a car accident with a drunk driver. I have had problems for two years and have lost all my shape and muscle tone. Recently I was able to start walking farther and have slowly started my descent down the cellulite ladder. I hope to be my old self by next year. I don't know if this man finds me attractive or if he is simply being a good friend. I do not want to approach him in my present condition; I'd rather be in good shape when I do.

My question is twofold. First, should I approach this man, make my feelings known, and hope he will wait for me, or do I just wait until I've shed some weight and approach him then, hoping he does not find someone else? And second, do you have any advice about how to approach him? I do not want to get my heart broken.

It sounds as if you have put a couple of important actions on hold for significant amounts of time. You are waiting to tell your parents that you are gay until you finish school and are no longer financially dependent on them, and you are waiting to tell someone that you are falling in love with him until you have lost a lot of weight and look like a much different person. The anxiety of waiting to accomplish these goals must be hard to bear, especially since you are telling yourself that completing the goals means doing two very stressful things: coming out to your parents and confessing your romantic feelings to your friend.

You sound like someone who could use some counseling, if only to reduce the level of stress in your life. You also need to figure out if these are things you really want to do or if you are simply postponing them because your subconscious knows there are perfectly good reasons to keep your mouth shut. Most universities offer free or low-cost therapy to their students. If this service exists at your school, take advantage of it.

Telling someone you have deep feelings for him is never easy. How you do it is not terribly important. If the other person shares your feelings, he will be delighted, whether you make your approach with a letter, E-mail, or signal flags or stutter it out in person. If he doesn't reciprocate, then he has the difficult task of telling you that without causing you undue pain. In my opinion, waiting will simply make it more difficult to get the words out.

You seem to assume that sex and romance are out of the question because you won't be attractive until your body changes in a major way. That assumption is worth a second look. Do you really want a boyfriend who is such an appearance snob that he can't remain bonded to you despite whatever health problems or imperfections life may bring? A counselor might be able to help you feel more self-acceptance and self-esteem. Feeling unworthy and second-rate will only make it harder to lose weight.

Only you can decide whether this is the right time to approach this man and see if he is interested in something besides friendship. But I think a broken heart is better than a heart in limbo. If someone rejects me, I can get over it. But if I don't ask, I put myself in a very anxious, paralyzed, blocked state of mind that takes the joy out of my life. If he says he wants to date and explore having a relationship with you, wouldn't that give you a powerful motivation to get back in shape? If I were you, I'd get a counselor to give me support in case I got bad news. Then I'd sit down and have an honest conversation with the one I adored.

75}

I understand the benefits derived from the scrotum's ability to draw the testicles close to the body. However, I don't need those benefits and would prefer the "loose" mode permanently. Can that be accomplished by surgery, by disconnecting one or two nerves without undue side effects? Or is it more involved than that? I don't want to stretch or distort my scrotum the way some apparatuses are designed to do; I'll be satisfied with my natural size if I can just get it to hang a little lower.

Besides the usual drawbacks to having your scrotum sawed open (temporary immobility, hideous scarring, insufferable pain and itching while you heal), there are plenty of reasons why you don't want to risk this sort of elective surgery—assuming you could find anyone willing to perform such an operation in the first place.

For starters, it just plain isn't safe to lop off tendons and ligaments for cosmetic reasons. Even if you're not planning to propagate, that stuff is there for a purpose. There's also the risk of nerve and circulatory damage. Although there have been no long-term studies done on the effects of such surgeries, a physician with whom I spoke thought that truncating your spermatic cord could affect your erectile capability—and he knew for a fact that your sperm count would fall through the floor.

Furthermore, there's the chance that the resulting formation of scar tissue could cause your testicles to retract, in which case your balls would end up hanging even closer to your body.

Gary Griffin of Added Dimensions Publishing, which specializes in books and devices designed to enlarge our parts (if not our minds), strongly recommends nonsurgical lengthening procedures. Pumps and weight systems are commonly used to achieve low-hangers, and although there are drawbacks to these methods as well, they're infinitely safer than any form of surgical intervention. You can write to Griffin at 100 S. Sunrise Way, Suite 484, Palm Springs, CA 92263. Please let him talk you into something other than having your nuts snipped.

76}

On a good day I stand all of five feet tall. I know it's politically correct to say that I'm "vertically challenged," but I prefer being called short. After years of therapy I have come to accept myself and my height as something that I have to deal with. But now that I've established that I prefer being with men (I used to date women and always went out with women taller than I am) and am out exploring my new gay life, I've encountered some problems.

Every time I go to a bar, I'm asked to show ID to prove my age (I'm 25). Then, once I'm inside, men pat me on the head and tell me how cute I am. I want to meet someone who thinks being short is hot, not someone who wants me merely because I pack a nice package below the waist (my dick is pretty big). So far I haven't had any luck meeting guys who are like me or prefer someone short. Any suggestions?

Don't underestimate the power of a nice package. You can, in certain settings, use the size you pack in your pants to make up for what you lack in stature.

In the meantime, it sounds as if you have a healthy attitude about your height. And since you happen to be one of those enormously fortunate men with that eternally youthful look, you can cash in on it by going after some nice guy who's looking for a "boy." Otherwise, you're left to seek out open-minded gay men to whom your size either is a turn-on or doesn't matter—because, unfortunately, there are no gay-specific organizations for people who live closer to the ground. Try placing a "romance" ad in your local gay paper in which you eschew elevator shoes and extol the heights of your wisdom and the joys of relative proportions. Good luck.

chapter 10

changes of pace (fetishes)

77}

Today at work I was caught by the UPS man with my mouth full. My lover of four years has been setting up these voyeuristic situations in which we're caught having sex, usually with his ample cock stuffed down my throat. He finds it very exciting and a true turn-on; I enjoy it because he enjoys it, and I tell him that I find it exciting too. But sometimes I feel that the people watching us think of me as subservient. Some have made comments after catching us, remarking that I can't seem to get enough dick. One of the maintenance workers even showed me his cock and said we should get together later. I have to admit, I thought about it. (His cock was fat and looked like it would be great to suck.)

Am I a dick pig for feeling this way? Should I just shut up and eat up or try to balance it all?

> This is a confusing letter. I can't tell from your description whether you feel used and degraded by your lover's fondness for workplace blow jobs or excited and intrigued by

the act of public sex. Maybe it's a little of both.

There's nothing wrong with liking a lot of sex, and doing the nasty in public is a major turn-on for a lot of guys. Your lover obviously gets off on being watched, and that's fine. Your concern seems to be with what those observers will think of you, not just for having gay sex in public but for always being the one on your knees. If that's all it is, just turn the tables a few times: Get caught with *your* dick in *his* mouth for a change. Then they'll talk about both of you equally.

If you're concerned about your overall reputation, though, you may wish to confine your antics to some public place outside the office. Gossip goes on in every workplace, and believe me, seeing a sight like the one you provide your coworkers is something that people will gossip about for a long time to come. (I know I would. Even here at *Unzipped* that kind of thing rarely happens.) Plus, you're risking the loss of your job—unless one of you is the boss, in which case you're risking possible complaints by employees to various meddlesome government agencies. (Though if you did it outside of work, you'd risk arrest, so pick your poison.)

This boils down to a matter of consent. You should not be forced to do anything you don't wish to do. If you feel degraded by servicing your boyfriend at work, then he shouldn't make you. But if you enjoy the sex and don't mind what people might say, then invest in some knee pads and slurp away.

78}

I've been doing S/M casually for a couple of years now. Lately, though, I've been having fantasies about deep submission. I really want to be a man's slave! I don't know any real masters or slaves, and a lot of the stories I read seem pretty unrealistic. The few D/S workshops I've seen listed are geared toward tops. How do I learn to be a good slave?

For the uninitiated, D/S stands for *dominance/submission*. Within the leather community, terms such as these—or, for that matter, *master* and *slave*—get thrown around a lot without much attempt at precise definition. I think what's most important right now is for you to be clear about what you think a fulfilling slave/master relationship would look like. It sounds as if you are looking for an emotional or physical experience that you have not found in casual S/M play. Defining that lack might be a good starting point for creating your paradigm of consensual sexual slavery. Start writing down exactly what seems unrealistic about the jack-off material you are reading. Then describe what you think a realistic alternative would be. A written account of this process will be fascinating reading for a master who wants to gain insight into your psychology. Of course, your fantasy will probably change and evolve as you encounter the needs of real-life masters and gain more experience in living out this role.

In the meantime, why not go to workshops, even if they are top-oriented? These events are a great way to meet masters or other slaves who might be able to give you advice and support. You need to know what masters are looking for, what their responsibilities are, and how to tell a man who knows safe technique from a guy who is too dangerous to trust in a scene. For people in the New York City area, I highly recommend Gay Male S/M Activists. You can write to them at 332 Bleecker St., Suite D23, New York, NY 10014, or call them at (212) 727-9878.

You might want to place an ad in *Bound and Gagged* ($30 for six issues to Outbound Press, 89 Fifth Ave., Suite 803, New York, NY 10003). This publication is for male bondage fans, but I have seen ads there for men interested in long-term restraint and servitude. For general information about the S/M scene, I recommend *Black Sheets* ($20 for four issues to The Black Book, P.O. Box 31155, San Francisco, CA 94131-0155). *Black Sheets* may be reached by phone at (800) 818-8823. This is a thoughtful pansexual leather publication that covers a lot of heretical philosophical territory.

And there are three other resources that might almost have been written specifically to answer your question. Jack

Rinella's *The Master's Manual: A Handbook of Erotic Dominance* (available from Daedalus Publishing Co., 584 Castro St., Suite 518, San Francisco, CA 94114; or you may E-mail Daedalus at 72114.2327@CompuServe.com) gives you one man's philosophy of the master/slave dynamic. It's a bit solemn for my taste, but Rinella is an experienced and sincere master, and there aren't many of those about. Much more frisky is Dossie Easton and Catherine A. Liszt's *The Bottoming Book: Or, How to Get Terrible Things Done to You by Wonderful People* (available from Lady Green, 3739 Balboa Ave., Suite 195, San Francisco, CA 94121). The title says it all. You could also benefit from a subscription to *The Servants' Quarters*, a 'zine devoted to the art of submission (four issues are $14 from Six of the Best Publishing, 2215-R Market St., Suite 264, San Francisco, CA 94114).

These publications can be obtained from Alamo Square Distributors, P.O. Box 14543, San Francisco, CA 94114. Send a self-addressed, stamped envelope for a free catalog. Alamo also carries the classic gay-male magazine on this topic, *Metropolitan Slave* ($32 for four issues, also available from Selective Publishing, P.O. Box 4597, Oak Brook, IL 60522-4597; Selective Publishing can be reached by phone at [708] 986-8550 or by E-mail at metroslave@aol.com). You can also get a free catalog of kinky books and magazines (if you're 21 or older) from QSM, P.O. Box 880154, San Francisco, CA 94188. QSM can be reached by phone at (415) 550-7776 or by E-mail at qsm@crl.com.

Of course, when ordering from any of these companies, be sure to include an over-18 age statement.

79}

Last night my boyfriend suggested hot wax as a way to spice up our sex lives. We have dabbled in some light S/M before but just with things like handcuffs and tit clamps, nothing too serious. Hot wax is something we'd never even thought of before now, and we don't really know where to begin with it. Are there any dangers we should know about, or can we just drip away? Can you offer some guidelines to ensure our safety?

Hot wax has long been a popular (and in terms of HIV, very safe) method of erotic play. How long? At least since your Adviser was in college back during the Truman administration, if you must know, smart-ass. And so long as you use common sense and don't set each other on fire, it's really tough to go wrong with it.

The best source of wax for sex play is common household candles. Just grab whatever you have stocked up in case the electricity goes out; they should work fine. One caution here, though: Don't use beeswax candles, as they burn at much higher temperatures than the normal variety and can easily burn the skin.

Before you start you may wish to shave whatever area of your or your lover's body you plan to drip wax on. When wax dries it can be very difficult and painful to remove from body hair. If you don't shave that body part, at least comb all the hair in one direction, which will make it easier to get the wax out. And if you do shave, remember that the newly bare area will be highly sensitive.

Wax should be dripped one drop at a time from a height of at least a foot (the higher you hold the candle, the more time the wax has to cool as it falls through the air). Never bring the actual flame into contact with the bottom's body; in fact, if he's hairy, don't even get it close. Also, don't allow liquid wax to run freely over the bottom's body, as it will puddle at his low points and could burn the skin. Normally the wax will not leave burns. A slight reddening of the skin is normal, but it should go away after a short while.

The effect this will have on the bottom is tough to describe. In one sense it is painful, but at the same time it's also…exquisite. Suffice it to say, he will experience some unique and intense sensations. (Needless to say, if he protests or finds it not to his liking, you should stop immediately.)

When you're done, the dried wax will peel off of bare skin or comb out of hairy skin. If the hair tangles, just cut it away from that particular area. Using wax to pull hair out is excruciatingly painful and should be left to women and vain guys who want to look good in bikinis.

80}

I recently moved to St. Croix in the Virgin Islands to work as a waiter during the winter tourist season. There is one gay bar here and one gay hotel, and so far it has been easy to arrange one-night stands with locals and tourists alike. The situation has been paradise.

I'm looking forward to having sex in the ocean or in a pool and have some questions about putting a condom on in the water. Should I put it on when I am already in the water, or should I put it on when I'm on dry land? What should I do about air pockets at the condom tip? What kind of lube should I use? It seems that a water-based lube would wash off right away. Is it OK to use an oil-based lube for this occasion? So far I've only skinny-dipped a few times with guys and played with their butts and cocks in the water. However, I want to go all the way. I hope you can help.

Of course I can help. I'm the Sex Adviser, aren't I? You have a couple of choices, not one of which should be taken lightly.

Your best bet is to don your condom before entering the

water. This way you'll avoid catching air bubbles between your cock and the condom that can stretch out the rubber and cause it to rupture. This will also prevent your urethra from filling with nasty salt water or chlorinated pool water, both of which can cause inflammation and discomfort.

Because you're in the water, you obviously won't be able to use water-based lubes after you're submerged. Before you get all wet, fill the condom with a lube that contains nonoxynol-9 (a spermicide that helps prevent HIV transmission) before you slip it on. Remember that water isn't as slick a substitute for lube as, say, saliva. Make sure your partner is good and ready before you slip it to him in the drink. And forget about using oil-based lubes now or any other time.

Finally, you could try my favorite: While standing in shallow water, wrap your arms around his neck and your legs around his waist. Lift yourself out of the water, lean back, and let him put the condom on you. (This one came to me while watching an old Esther Williams musical.)

By the way, your life sounds like a dream come true. Good for you.

81}

Drag is something that simply fascinates me. While I've never seriously tried it, I am in love with the fabulous world of the drag queen. I used to dress up in my mother's clothes when I was young, and the interest has carried over to this day. I am obsessed with cross-dressers, transsexuals, and transvestites. I would like to know where to find a magazine about men who dress like women. I'd prefer a magazine with listings of nightclubs and other places where I can meet these kinds of interesting people. Is there such a thing?

Is there such a thing? Is there ever! Race right down to your neighborhood kiosk and check out the latest issues of *Transgender Tapestry*, *LadyLike*, and the extremely popular *Dragazine*, edited by drag superstar Lois Commondenominator. Each of these glamorous glossies is bursting with photographs of men in dresses and filled with stories about which bustier is best.

If your newsstand is bereft of these provocative periodicals, you can contact them and request sample issues. *Transgender Tapestry* is at (617) 899-2212, and if you can't get the editors of *LadyLike* on the phone at (610) 640-9449, try their Web page at www.cdspub.com. You can write to *Dragazine* at P.O. Box 461795, West Hollywood, CA 90046.

You go, girl.

82}

Can you give me advice about a sexual desire of mine? I wonder if this sort of sexual manipulation will cause me medical problems later in life. I consider myself normal, having a seven-inch cock and average-size balls. What turns me on is to pull my cock up between my legs and push my balls into their inner cavity. This excites me no end. I have no desire to be a woman or to have my manhood surgically removed.

I have created a contraption (which took endless hours to develop) with laces and tape so I can pull my penis up between my legs, pop my nuts into their inner cavity, and tie it off so that everything stays perfectly snug. I'll then dress as usual and put a sock in my underwear to make everything normal-looking. I'll then go about my business as if nothing is amiss. I don't leave my cock pulled up too long, as I'm afraid of cutting off blood circulation and damaging my nuts. I feel no pain; it's just a great turn-on. Getting a hard-on this way feels awesome.

I want to spring this habit of mine on my boyfriend, then have him fuck me while my cock is tied up between my legs. I also want to wear it for long periods of time this way. My question to you is this: Will continuing this activity impact my manhood in any way?

Picture your adviser doubled up in imagined pain as he answers this one.

Gay rights activists have been banging their heads against walls for decades in order that you and I may put our cocks and balls anyplace we like—including up inside ourselves. But there are several things you should know before continuing your little vanishing act.

There are handy gadgets, available through most leather shops and at some adult-novelty boutiques, that will truss you up efficiently and relatively safely. These devices, usually made of leather, will no doubt lift and tuck you more prudently than your tape-and-string gizmo. Also, several mail-order companies that cater to female impersonators carry mysterious underthings that mash even the most awesome endowment into a tidy little package.

Regardless of how sophisticated the apparatus you use, however, it's important that you not leave your "things" tied up too long. Cutting off the circulation of blood to any part of your body, much less the genitals, can cause irreparable harm. Make sure that you're doing this as infrequently as you can bear and for only short periods of time.

And you should probably first discuss this peculiar passion of yours with your boyfriend before springing it on him unawares. Unless you've bagged an especially sympathetic guy, he may bolt at the sight of a dickless queer. After all, a gay man without a cock is sort of like a Mae West impersonator without a big, flouncy hat.

83}

I'm a 29-year-old man who's attracted to good-looking guys as much as the next gay man, but I have what I guess could be considered a very unusual fetish. I find a very masculine neck extremely arousing, especially a nice, prominent Adam's apple. There is just something about that particular area of the male anatomy that excites me and is extremely sexually stimulating.

My idea of a fantasy lover is a guy who would allow me to fulfill my greatest secret desire, which is to have him lie back and let me see his Adam's apple up close and to kiss it and explore its size and shape with my index finger and tongue.

I have had these feelings for as long as I can remember, but I've kept them to myself out of fear of rejection or embarrassment. Is this a common type of fetish, or am I all alone?

No, you are not the only Adam's apple fetishist. There are two others, both of whom have contacted me recently asking for photographs of your neck.

Seriously, there is nothing wrong with sexual fixations so long as they aren't doing you or anyone else any harm. And while there are probably fewer men enamored of Adam's apples than of, say, feet or armpits, I think most of us have an affinity for one part of the anatomy or another.

Fetishism is usually about the imprinting we do in our early, formative years. For example, if the only attention we ever got from men was when our dads spanked us, we very well may have eroticized that and today can get off only if an older man takes a hairbrush to our behinds and tells us we've been naughty.

There are those who believe that fetishism can be carried to extremes, that when we're able to get off only if our partner is a six-foot blond brandishing a whip and wearing a dirndl (or whatever), we're limiting the kinds of sexual experiences we can have. But there's nothing wrong with focusing on one individual part of a man's anatomy. There's doubtless someone out there who wants more than anything to meet a man who will worship his Adam's apple. Get out there and find him.

84}

Recently I got one of those shower douche gadgets that diverts water through a hose up your butt. I have two questions: First, since this device came with no directions, are there guidelines—besides trial and error—about what is safe in terms of volume of water, rate of inflow, and temperature? Second, is there a limit to how many times one can douche per week without ill effects?

Men who thrill to drinking from both ends should fill themselves with knowledge first. There's nothing hot about drowning—recall Shelley Winters in *The Poseidon Adventure*? Enemas of plain water or water and phosphate salts are safe unless you're suffering from appendicitis or diverticulitis. As a result of these conditions, your already inflamed bowel muscles will contract against the load you've forced up there, which can cause at least violent pain and at worst a perforation of the colon.

An enema of plain water requires no chaser; soap is an irritant that can damage the lining of the colon to such an extent that severe abdominal pain and rectal bleeding may occur.

Fluids that you put up inside yourself should be no warmer than your normal body temperature, and you should never put more of anything up your butt than you can take without pain (no matter how chiseled his features). Like the box office returns from *Waterworld*, inflow should be slow and steady. You don't want to rupture anything.

Keep in mind that frequent or prolonged use of enemas may result in dependence. An enema interrupts the natural action of the colon—the salt and fluid cause the colon to contract and evacuate your bowels. Make sure that you aren't relying on your favorite Esther Williams fantasies to maintain a regular bowel habit.

85}

At the leather club I belong to, each of us practices safe sex. Some of us are really into sex toys, and each uses only his own toys. None are shared. Some of us have really gotten into the new electric toys, such as electric butt plugs, electric sparklers, and electric cock rings that are advertised in the leather publications. My question is this: Is there a serious health risk in passing an electrical current through the body? Does it weaken the immune system or raise the risk of prostate problems? Or is it just great, safe fun?

All electrical play is risky to some extent. Some people in the S/M community who are experienced with electrical play suggest that you can make it safer by using equipment that is battery-operated rather than equipment that plugs into a wall outlet. Electrical toys that obtain their power from house circuits contain transformers that step down the current to protect you from being exposed to any unexpected blasts of power. If these transformers should fail, however, you could get a dangerous shock from the toy. This can't happen with battery-operated equipment. These experts also caution people against running current across the chest (from nipple to nipple, for example), since this could potentially affect the heartbeat.

Your other questions are much more difficult to answer. No research has been done about the influence of electrical toys on the immune system or on the prostate gland. However, some environmentalists and health workers are asking questions about electromagnetic fields (EMFs). Computer manufacturers in Sweden are required to produce machines that will not expose office workers to certain levels of EMFs. This country has not taken much action in this area. This might be a good starting point for you to do some reading and figure out what is an acceptable level of risk for you. However, the research on EMFs is very technical and hard to follow. It is also not conclusive.

Whether power lines and electrical appliances cause cancer or other health problems is not yet established. Even if you believe that EMFs are harmful and that people should strive to reduce their exposure, I wonder whether an electrical toy would increase EMF exposure to a clinically significant degree for someone who lives with not only a refrigerator, CD player, TV, VCR, home computer, food processor, microwave oven, and electric lights but also outdoor power cables. Your toys are probably about as dangerous as a recliner with a massage unit.

Sorry I can't be more definitive. Given the ubiquity of electricity, it's very possible that adequate research on this issue will never be funded.

86}

Because of a fear of HIV, I have not had any sexual relationships during the past eight years. However, I do have phone sex, and for the past five years or so I've allowed other men to put my phone number up in bookstores, at truck stops, and on bathroom walls to facilitate this. One of my many fantasy trips is having a stranger pose as a bill collector and call me to demand payment for a nonexistent bill. On many occasions I have sent payment, and sometimes I keep this game going for up to two months. Since most of the calls are collect, I usually have a big phone bill, but I seem to desire having to pay for these JO calls.

Do I need professional help, or is this just a long phase I'm going through that will eventually pass?

At the very least, you should be commended for practicing such safe sex. It doesn't get much safer than your phone fantasies—unless one of these "bill collectors" sends some goons over to bust your kneecaps for being delinquent.

Whether this is a problem depends on your financial circumstances. If you are well-off enough to spend whatever it is you're spending without incurring undue financial hardship, then I say go for it. Lots of guys like phone sex, and there's nothing wrong with being creative about it. Anything you can do to make it more interesting is to your credit.

However, if you are spending more on these phone games than you can reasonably afford, you might have a problem. If you find that this is the case and that you cannot cut back voluntarily, I suggest counseling. There are many mental health resources in a city the size of yours; you might start with a group for sexual compulsives.

Only you can make the determination.

87}

I like—no, I love—cock and ball accessories: cock straps, cock rings, shaft rings, ball dividers, ball separators (yes, there is a difference), ball stretchers, ball lifters (great for advertising your equipment under jeans), and the like. Metal ones, leather ones, rubber ones—I know and love them all. I wear them all and have for some time.

Therein lies my question. Once in a moment of stupidity I wore a cock strap to my doctor's office for an examination. When he saw it he launched into a lecture about the hazards of such equipment. I can't remember all of the horrors he listed, but having your testicles explode from restricted blood flow was about the least horrendous.

Is this sound advice? My doctor is gay, but that doesn't mean he's immune to society's bigotries and misconceptions about sexual practices. I never wear these things to sleep in (things start to throb after you've rolled over on them a couple of times), but I frequently wear them under my clothes during the day (usually just a rubber cock ring, but sometimes others, separately or together).

Am I endangering myself? I wouldn't do this if it hurt. Surprising as it may be given the uses some people put these devices to, I'm not into pain.

I doubt that I would completely give up my addiction to cock and ball wear—once you've experienced the heightened sensitivity caused by a just-tight-enough cock strap and shaft ring, you'll never settle for an unenhanced erection again! But I would like to know the real health risks.

Wearing a cock strap to your doctor's office wasn't an act of stupidity after all—it may have preserved your health, not to mention your dick.

Although continued use of your favorite sex toys may not risk your life, it can harm your limbs if you're restricting blood flow to your cock and balls. Anytime you cut off the flow of oxygen and blood to any part of your body for long periods of time, you're asking for trouble. Blood carries waste products away from body parts and nourishes them with oxygen. Without consistent blood flow, cells can't reproduce, and any organ or limb that isn't replicating cells or receiving necessary oxygen is in big danger. Your dick may be bigger and better in your favorite adornments, but nobody will want to play with it after it rots and falls off.

Exercise a little caution. Wear your straps and separators for a couple of hours at a time—maybe before you go out to score and during sex play. Otherwise, leave them on the nightstand. Think of them as neckties—you wouldn't wear your favorite cravat to the local leather bar, would you?

88}

As an unattached 30-year-old gay man, I am always exploring new ways to experience my sexuality. Recently my interests and fantasies have included autofellatio. I find myself looking for scenes in X-rated videos, searching the magazine racks for pictorials, and surfing the Internet in search of others who share my obsession. More and more I find that, through consistent yoga stretching exercises, I am able to successfully masturbate myself orally. I wonder: Is there a magazine or club that is devoted to the world of autofellatio?

Lucky you. If all gay men possessed this skill, romance would probably go the way of the *lambada*.

There are a fistful of resources for those who want to emulate your unique talent. Gary Griffin's *The Art of Auto Fellatio* ($11.95 from Added Dimensions Publishing, 100 S. Sunrise Way, Suite 484, Palm Springs, CA 92263) is the bible, as it were, of the autofellating set. Griffin's book is thick with step-by-step instructions on how to reach your potential and crowded with photographs of others doing the same. The book also includes a directory of some 70 videos and magazines featuring self-suckers. The magazine *Penis Power Quarterly*, also published by Added Dimensions ($24.95 for a one-year subscription), sometimes features stories on men who can fold themselves in half. Unfortunately, there's no news of a club for autofellators, though just the thought of what a membership meeting might look like has your Adviser bent double.

chapter 11

the sex industry

89}

I live in a rural area about 400 miles from any major cities. I'm over 40 and still have my looks, and I want to live out some of my fantasies. Specifically, I want to hire a "masseur" or an "escort." What are the best cities for procuring them? Also, how do I make sure I'm going to get what I'm asking for before putting out all that money? I don't have any friends I can ask for advice or information. How do I read between the lines of the ads in various publications? What is the going rate for services?

The ads in *Unzipped* for escorts and masseurs offer services that are safe and legal. There's nothing unlawful about buying a good, hard rubdown or the company of a nice young man to have dinner and maybe a midnight swim with.

If one of your fantasies is to receive an hour-long massage from a hunky man wearing only construction boots and a hard hat, you're in luck. Anything that transpires between you and the gentleman in question after you conclude your business is entirely your affair, so to speak. Perhaps you'll take a liking to him and want to buy him a new pair of shoes. Perhaps he'll want you to clean his old pair using only your tongue. Who am I to say?

Whatever you do, it's probably wise to determine beforehand what you're paying for. If you've hired a nude maid to dust your trinkets, you may want to know if his price also includes cleaning your oven. Ask him about this *before* he whips out his feather duster to ensure that you will be getting the most for your money.

Prices will probably vary depending on where you're buying and whether or not the talent you're hiring has an agent. Models tend to get paid more for photo shoots in Manhattan, for example, than in Paducah. In the theater, matinees often cost less than evening performances, and we can assume that the actors would charge us even more if they had to come to our homes to perform.

Some towns don't have a playhouse, however. There's plenty of theater in New York and Los Angeles; therefore, there are probably more hungry actors there than anyplace else. But with a little careful digging, you can usually find a Chippendales wanna-be in any major city.

Regardless of your locale, no one—your Adviser included—should recommend that you do anything outside the law. If you're thinking of doing something illegal, take a cold shower and eat a carton of ice cream instead. (I'm eating a tub of jamocha ripple right this minute, but you can bet I'm thinking about a hunky masseur.)

90}

I am 18 years old. I just graduated from high school and have no plans for my future. I've got no money, no way to travel, and nothing to do but sit here and read. I live on a farm in Ohio and have no contacts with anyone anywhere, but I very much want to get into gay porn, which has always really turned me on. I'm bored here and want to get out and enjoy life and make my mark. I can't tell my parents I'm gay; they are very antigay and would probably shoot me or at least kick me out. I don't know how I survived this long with them. I know I'm the only gay person for miles around, and I don't know what to do. Can you suggest something?

Let me begin by congratulating you for having survived in such an antigay, hate-filled environment. It's certainly been an unpleasant space for you to grow up in, and I commend you for having stuck it out. So many gay teens opt out by offing themselves; I'm always pleased to hear about any young gay person who has persevered and is ready to move on.

But before you do, think hard about what you plan to do.

The porn business is a difficult trade to break into and one that provides a lot to very few. As with many forms of show business, there's room for only a few superstars, and those who fall short of that coveted status have to work twice as hard for half as much. It probably looks like making sex videos is a lot of fun, but there's a lot more to it than fucking and sucking and collecting a paycheck. Most porn performers have day jobs of one sort or another. A small minority of established stars make a living from merchandising and personal appearances, but most have other careers that are considerably less glamorous. According to the porn stars I've spoken to, there's very little glamour in their business, and there's an awful lot of sitting around between shots, so to speak, on any porn flick. It's not as easy as you might think to get it up and keep it up while cameramen find the right angles for a sex scene. Being paid to fuck someone beautiful for the whole world to see may sound like a dream come true, but consider this: You're surrounded by a film crew, you have to screw the poor fellow for several hours, and you can't come until the director decides he has enough footage of you and your actor pal. My balls ache just thinking about this. I'm not saying porn is something you shouldn't do, but please think hard about it and know what you're getting into before you try it.

And while you're thinking about it, why not look for work in some nearby city? After several months of waiting tables or working in the steel mill, you'll have saved enough to get yourself an apartment and can really begin your new, out gay life with style. Meanwhile, keep your porn collection carefully hidden from your parents.

91}

I'm a 34-year-old man who can't stand the thought of going to my job one more day. I've worked in the same place for the past 11 years, and it's time for a change. The thing that I would most like to do is direct gay erotic videos. Most of my friends think I just want to be around good-looking naked men, and although that is a plus, it's not the only reason. I honestly think a lot of the videos out there are just plain junk with absolutely no story.

But how does one start directing gay erotic videos? I'm sure even Chi Chi LaRue had to start somewhere. If you could give me some advice, I'd really appreciate it.

As with any business, breaking into the porn world is, to some degree, about whom you know. To a surprisingly large extent, though, it's also about what you know.

Most of the top directors in this business started out in the porn industry in some other capacity. LaRue, for one, started in a much less glamorous position, doing sales and promotions for companies such as Catalina, and then schmoozed and self-promoted his way to the top through good people skills and tireless devotion to his craft. The fact that he knew both gay and straight porn inside and out didn't hurt either.

While LaRue and others learned a lot of what makes them good directors on the job, you can't just land a directing gig as a rank amateur these days. Some porn background or film or theater training is a must.

Falcon's much-respected John Rutherford tutored under the legendary Steven Scarborough, who's now at Hot House. Jerry Douglas, whose *Flesh and Blood* swept Best Video honors at last year's Gay Erotic Video and Adult Video News awards, is a Yale-trained dramatist. Mike Donner of All Worlds has a theater background as well. Others—New Age's Gino Colbert and Centaur's Chip Daniels are two successful examples—actually performed on-camera before moving behind it.

The point is, no one's going to just hire you off the street to direct porn. You need to get a foot in the door somewhere in a less glamorous position, then try to work your way up. Unless you're already well-versed in things like lighting, camera angles, timing, spacing, and how to direct dialogue, then even in this business you'll have to pay your dues.

If you're concerned about story lines, try writing a screenplay and submitting it around. But if you think everything out today is thin on plot, you must have missed Douglas's *Flesh and Blood*, Donner's *Our Trespasses*, LaRue's *Lost in Vegas*, and most of the other top films of 1996.

92}

I have a very serious problem: I am obsessed with porn stars Chuck Barron and Danny Somers. I am totally serious when I say that my life has been severely affected by this obsession. As I am completely preoccupied with thoughts of these two beautiful men, my job performance has suffered, and my current relation-ship is on the rocks, as I no longer find it fulfilling. My lover is jealous of two porn stars we have never met. (And I can't blame him, because I have feelings for them that my feelings for him do not approach.)

The fact is, I find Chuck Barron to be my dream man, and it's not just about sex. I am fascinated by his voice, his demeanor, and his body language. There are other men in porn who are bet-ter-built, better-hung, and better-looking, but the sexual chem-istry between Chuck and Danny makes me feel like they would be my perfect soul mates.

I am intrigued by Danny as well, though not quite to the same extent. My ultimate fantasy would be to be in a long-term relationship with both of these guys at the same time. It seems absurd, but it is beyond sex—it is love. I am devoted to both of these guys already without ever having touched or spoken to them. I would do anything to make them happy.

I am not completely irrational. I know it's very unlikely that I will ever meet either of these guys, much less be in a loving (or even just sexual) relationship with even one of them. This is the problem: I don't think I'll ever be happy or fulfilled in a relationship with anyone else. Always in the back of my mind—while working, making love, or doing anything else—I will be thinking of Chuck and Danny.

Actually, I find it depressing, because I feel that I can live only half a life apart from them. Don't suggest therapy, because only Chuck's embrace or Danny's kisses could make me feel otherwise.

Do you think it's possible for three people to be in a serious long-term relationship at the same time and love one another equally?

Possibly, but that's not the issue you should be concerned about. The real question is how you can quit pining away for two guys you've never met and get on with some semblance of a normal life.

Let's define our terms first. While your feelings are doubtlessly very strong, I don't believe that what you are feeling is love. You cannot fall in love with a person you've never met. Love at first sight is a fantasy product of Hollywood movies and romance novels, and that's fine. But in real life what you are dealing with in initial impressions is physical attraction. That's enough to start with, but real love grows only over time: when you establish compatibility; when you're comfortable together; when you can spend an evening together without running out of things to say; when you get to know a person's likes, dislikes, strengths, weaknesses, and eccentricities; and when you get to know all of their faults, even their darkest sides, and accept them and care for them anyway.

You have fallen for two attractive physical exteriors without any knowledge of what's underneath. Chuck Barron and Danny Somers may be very fine, decent people, or they may, underneath it all, be raging assholes. For the sake of argument, what if they're thieving, alcoholic, physically abusive polecats? What if they're mean to puppies and small children? What if their sexual preferences include livestock? (I'm not saying this is the case; I've never met either one of them either.) Can you see the folly of assigning them all of these wonderful characteristics in your fantasies without knowing the reality?

So let's say you're infatuated. Infatuations can be very intense and sometimes more debilitating than actual love. This is precisely because you're not seeing the raw, unvarnished reality. You have painted a perfect fantasy in your mind to which reality can never measure up. Even if you meet Chuck and Danny, the likelihood that they're going to be just like you imagine them is slim. All of us have flaws, yet your preconceptions of them have set a standard of perfection.

It would be interesting to know more of your romantic

history—specifically, if you've had a history of problematic relationships or setting your sights on unattainable men. Fantasies are fine, but I wonder if there's an underlying reason for what you're experiencing now. Maybe you've been hurt before and are subconsciously gravitating toward men who won't hurt you again. Maybe you want to be hurt and are selecting men you know you can never have. Maybe you're afraid of intimacy and need a barrier (like, say, 1,500 miles) between you and the object of your desires. There could be any number of subtle psychological factors at play here, if you're ever interested in exploring them with a professional.

In general, when people write to me lusting after porn stars, I tell them to quit sitting at home whacking off to pretty pictures and to get out there and meet some real men. If your boyfriend doesn't push your buttons in a way that makes you forget about these unattainable icons, the same advice probably applies to you. It's unfair to waste his time if you're going to be mooning like a lovesick adolescent over someone else. And you need someone—in the flesh—who can set your heart afire too. But whatever you decide to do—getting counseling, finding a new boyfriend—do something. Your current obsession is a recipe for an unhappy life.

chapter 12

miscellaneous

93}

I have often wondered if it is possible to make homemade dildos. I work in a gay and lesbian bookshop in Texas, where such items are not available in local retail outlets—they are illegal. Mail order is done at your own risk. Any information (such as what type of materials are used to make molds and to cast the dildo so that it is usable) that could be passed along by you would be greatly appreciated.

The materials and skills that you need are readily available from shops and classes that cater to model makers, woodworkers, doll makers, and other hobbyists. It is fairly simple to carve a dildo out of soft balsa wood. You can also go to a hardware store and buy dowels the width of a broomstick (or however thick you want them), cut them into sections, and carve those, although they are made out of slightly harder wood. The problem with wood dildos is that they are porous (which makes them hard to clean), hard, and slightly abrasive (which makes them a little difficult for tender assholes to tolerate). You should carefully sand and then finish your toy with the sort of nontoxic oil that is used to finish cutting boards. Even so, it should probably be a one-person toy and should be used with a condom to make sure the surface is smooth. If you'd like a slightly more "cushy" feel, wrap quilt batting or a thin layer of foam rubber around your dildo, glue it in place, and cover it with several condoms.

You can use your wooden model (or sculpt your ideal dick out of clay) to make a plaster cast in two parts. That can then be used as a mold that can be filled with liquid plastic, latex, or silicone. Any large hobby shop or art supply store should have books about making molds. Liquid latex is available at theatrical makeup companies. Most plastics supply places will have silicone. Be sure to check out how toxic the chemicals in question are, since the lining of your butt readily absorbs whatever touches it. You can tell the salesclerk you are making toys for children and want to be sure that they are safe and can be chewed.

An ancient alternative is to simply use fresh produce of the appropriate size. Wash to remove pesticides, then cover with a condom. And finally, be aware that large pet supply stores and some veterinary catalogs sell "dog retrieval dummies" that look amazingly much like something else.

94}

The word *guiche* keeps appearing in the various adult magazines I read. The word is not in any dictionary that I can find. Please, will you define it for me? Where is it? What's it used for? How do you pronounce it? Is it fun? Can I get one? Should I ask my mother to knit one for me?

Alas, the failings of Mr. Webster. A guiche (pronounced like "quiche," for those of you who appreciate brunch references in your discussions of body modification) is a body piercing in which a thick ring (or, less commonly, a bar) is placed through the perineum, the area of skin between the scrotum and the asshole. This type of piercing was frequently sported by men in Polynesian and other island nations, although the exact cultural significance of it in those societies is unclear.

In addition to simply being visually interesting, a guiche can be sexually arousing. Because of the perineum's location beneath the prostate gland, pulling on a guiche or attaching weights to it can be very pleasurable. Like any body piercing, a guiche must be kept clean to prevent infection, and it is not recommended for people who frequently ride horses, bicycles, or motorcycles or who engage in activities involving prolonged contact between the guiche and a seat.

95}

Here is a problem I've never seen addressed in your column: I'm in the process of changing my sex from male to female. I've already started preliminary treatments, though I won't have the final surgery for some time yet. I am seeing a therapist about all the issues that accompany this life change, but can you give me some practical advice as to how I go about registering my new identity for tax, Social Security, and other governmental purposes? I'd hate to have trouble with the IRS in addition to everything else!

Call your Sex Adviser a pessimist, but he's learned to expect the worst in dealing with the government. He sincerely hopes you aren't getting the whole new you into a lifetime of tax headaches and conflicts with truculent DMV employees.

The first thing you'll want to do, according to some general guidelines I located on the Web, is obtain a Social Security card bearing your new name. To do this you'll have to show the folks at your local Social Security office either one piece of identification showing both your old and new names or two separate documents, one with your old name and one with your new one. Forms of ID acceptable for this purpose include your driver's license or state ID, passport, marriage or divorce certificate, school ID, insurance records, doctor's records (a note from your therapist may suffice), military records, or a court order for your name change. Birth certificates are not acceptable, nor are copies—even notarized ones. Social Security will need the original document or a certified copy from the county official who keeps your records.

Driver's license changes are more problematic, and the procedure will vary by state. You should contact your local office to determine what documents they'll require.

In both of these instances, bear in mind that you're changing your name only. Your sex will need to be changed in official records as well. Change it with Social Security first, since Social Security records can be used to change other records. You can simply mark your new sex when you fill out your name-change application and hope they don't give you static; if they do, you should refer them to your therapist. (Give your therapist written permission to discuss your case for this purpose. Patient confidentiality will prohibit him or her from doing it otherwise, and a verbal OK is not good enough.)

96}

Why do gay people have to do so many drugs to have a good time? I have been out for several years and have dated many different men in many different cities. Yet everywhere I go, this seems to be the case.

We do drugs, you see, because we are a vapid, uninteresting lot and because we require as much stimulation as possible in order to fully enjoy ourselves. Judging from your charming *Lion King* stationery, I sense that you're a guy who knows how to have a good time without the aid of Seconal and a spoonful of blow.

OK, enough with the sarcasm. Your question is sensible and one that many of us would benefit from asking more often. Although there's no easy answer to why a comparatively large number of gay men abuse drugs and alcohol, the most popular theory among psychotherapists points to our own self-hatred.

Drug abuse, many believe, is a symptom of internalized

homophobia. Gay men who are uncomfortable being gay find that they're better able to cope with their sexuality when they're anesthetized. Likewise, it's easier for some gay men to act on their sexual desires when they've ingested a handful of cat tranquilizers—or whatever—and are therefore "not themselves" while they're functioning sexually.

Also, the way that gay men are usually socialized has something to do with our affinity for drug use. We often enter gay social circles via gay bars, which for a very long time were the only places where queers could meet in a social environment. Hanging out in bars leads to drinking, and drinking often leads to other substance use, and pretty soon, if you're not careful, you've got a chemical dependency.

I'm tempted to quote Nancy Reagan here, but instead I'll say this: There are more fulfilling habits one can acquire. If you haven't already become addicted to crystal meth, why not try dishing your best friends' attire, collecting Julie Andrews records, or authoring a gay sex-advice column?

97}

I'm in a mixed relationship. I guess most people would think that this means we are of different races or that one of us is HIV-positive and the other is HIV-negative. Not so. My boyfriend is in Recovery, and I do mean that with a capital *R*. He goes to some kind of 12-step meeting every single day. If he's had a bad day, he goes to more than one. Sometimes this means he cancels dates with me.

I honestly can't see what he is getting out of these meetings that makes this obsession worthwhile. He has his life together—good job, nice apartment, caring friends, and me, crazy in love with him. I can't see any sign of alcoholism or any other kind of addiction in him except for this addiction to meetings. If he wants me, I guess we will continue to become more involved, but I don't want to be a 12-step widow. Is there any possibility that his craze will wane as time passes? (He's been clean and sober for five years.)

Have you ever asked your boyfriend what his life was like before he started going to all these meetings? Chances are, before he got sober he wasn't somebody you would have wanted to know, much less have for a lover. Active addiction consumes a huge amount of the addict's time, energy, and resources. In comparison, even one or two meetings a day take up a mere sliver of one's life. I frequently hear people who are not "in program" complain that 12-steppers are "addicted to their meetings." If you've experienced the financial chaos, emotional insecurity, claustrophobia, and desperation of being addicted to alcohol or some other drug, this label seems very cruel and inaccurate. I suppose in some sense you could say that diabetics are "addicted" to insulin. But it would be insane for someone with a disease to quit taking prescribed medication. An addict who wants to clean up has to make sobriety a priority.

Your man has gotten back on his feet and found a system that works for him. Don't tamper with it unless you want to go through a relapse with all its attendant guilt, sorrow, rage, and fear. Instead of viewing his meetings as time he takes away from you and your relationship, think of them as something he does to make your relationship possible. The love he has for you surely has to be one of the things that motivates him to keep working a program.

You don't say whether you have ever been to a meeting yourself. Why not sit in on an Alcoholics Anonymous or Narcotics Anonymous meeting or two? The stories you hear will definitely help you to understand where your lover is coming from. Since you can't throw anything at me, I will also suggest you think about a program for the partners of addicts, such as Al-Anon or Nar-Anon. This would be a healthy way to keep your partner's addiction (which is like a disease in remission) from controlling your life. If nothing else, you would find a sympathetic audience for a little bitching about the postponed dates and "12-step widow" syndrome.

98}

This column may not be meant for this kind of question, but I'm too embarrassed to ask anyone I know about this. I recently started working out at a health club, and one of my favorite things to do there is ride the stationary bike. The problem is that after about 15 minutes of riding, my penis keeps "falling asleep." I have tried to use different seats but have met with the same results. I don't really mind its happening ("waking up" can be rather interesting), but I am wondering whether it is harmful. I don't use that piece of my personal equipment a lot, but I want it to be in good working order when I need it. If this "falling asleep" is harmful, is there anything I can do to keep myself "awake"? I've tried moving around a lot to keep the blood flowing, but even that doesn't seem to help. What can I do?

I'm assuming that when you say your penis "falls asleep," you mean that you get a numb feeling or a tingling sensation in it. If so, it simply means there isn't enough blood flowing through the area. This could be caused by a number of things. My first thought is that perhaps whatever kind of underwear or workout shorts you're wearing is just too tight around the crotch and is cutting off blood flow in that area when you sit. If you're wearing a jock, maybe the straps are too tight and it's cutting into your crotch. Perhaps you should try wearing something looser to see if that clears up the problem. Another possibility is that the front of the bicycle seat is simply pressing tightly against the blood vessels in your crotch when you sit down, thereby cutting off circulation.

Whatever the reason, it sounds as if this happens only when you sit on the bicycle seat and not at any other time. As long as you aren't in pain and it isn't affecting your ability to urinate or ejaculate, I really wouldn't worry about it. It sounds as though it's just one of those odd things that happens. And, as you say, "waking yourself up" can be a great way to end your workout.

99}

I am a 33-year-old gay black male. I used to be happy that I was gay. As time has gone by, however, I've found that the only masculine qualities I have are physical; my personality is very feminine. And I have found that men don't like that. Guys tell me that if they wanted a woman, they'd be with a real one. The problem is that I am real; there's nothing fake about me. I love my qualities—they make up who I am. Yet I haven't found that special someone for me. I know what I can offer and how to please and satisfy a man, so what am I doing wrong? Will I ever be accepted for being myself and not what other men want me to be?

I really believe that there's someone out there for everyone, so if you haven't found your soul mate yet, just keep looking. It may seem as if you're not getting anywhere, and it may be discouraging at times, but if you persevere, it's bound to happen eventually.

It is true that pronounced feminine behavior is a turnoff

for a lot of gay men. It also stands to reason, though, that there are guys for whom it is a turn-on (and, by the same logic, a good number of guys who don't care one way or the other).

If you're looking for a life partner, you'll want to be judged by what's inside of you—your personality, your character, your values—not by outer mannerisms that may be effeminate. Guys who judge you only by these mannerisms aren't looking deep within you, and they aren't likely to be what you're looking for in a partner. A good prospect will get to know the real you, and that must happen before you can bond for life.

Putting on a facade won't get you anything beyond a onetime screw with someone who thinks you're something you're not. Your best chance for happiness is to be yourself and let the guys you meet get to know the real you. I'm sorry there aren't any easier answers; people seem to think the Sex Adviser has some secret for meeting the perfect man, and there simply isn't one. There are no quick and foolproof methods to marital bliss. You just have to maximize your opportunities and hang in there until it happens.

100}

I am 18 and live with my cabbie dad, who plays cards every week with his buddies. One night one of them brought a motorcycle-cop "friend" with him, and this guy lost a lot of money to my dad. Well, the next day, while my dad was out, this guy decided to get back at my dad through me. He came over and handcuffed me to the back of his bike, then took me to his dungeon, where he took his clippers and shaved my head.

As it turned out, this "friend" was someone my father's buddy had met in a bar, and he hasn't been seen since. As for me, I'm still as bald as the day he did this, and that was four months ago. Apparently my hair is not going to grow back.

Do you know of any other guys this has happened to? Although the humiliation was intense and being bald has really hurt me emotionally, I still get a hard-on when I see a cop on a motorcycle.

This has to be one of the most interesting letters I've ever received. There could be any number of reasons why your hair has not grown back, so my first suggestion is to get to a doctor, probably a dermatologist, and get yourself checked out in case there's a medical problem.

What I think is more likely is that you are experiencing some kind of lingering emotional or psychological scarring from this ordeal. (Can this actually stop your hair from growing? Beats me; that's why you should see a doctor.) If your hair grew normally before and has stopped growing only since this traumatic incident, there's probably a link. Counseling may be called for. The fact that you are attaching erotic feelings to motorcycle cops now seems to indicate that this affected you on some levels deeper than just your scalp. You need to explore these feelings in greater depth with a trained professional.

There is also the fact that what this guy did to you involves kidnapping and assault, both serious crimes. If you did not report it to the (real) police then, you should do so now. If you can find your way back to this guy's dungeon, justice should be reasonably easy to attain. Even if he's moved by now, there should be enough of a paper trail that the authorities can track him down. Your rights have been seriously violated, so don't take this lying down.

In the meantime, until the docs can get your pate repaired, slap a wig on it. And tell your dad and his friend to be more careful about who they hang out with; it could have been much, much worse for you.